REDBOOK'S
WISE
WOMAN'S
DIET
AND EXERCISE
BOOK

REDBOOK'S WISE WOMAN'S DIET AND EXERCISE BOOK

By the Editors of REDBOOK

The McCall Publishing Company

NEW YORK

Published simultaneously in Canada by Doubleday Canada Ltd., Toronto.

Library of Congress Catalog Card Number: 76–128144

SBN 8415–0068–1

Illustrations by Blaine Saunders

PRINTED IN THE UNITED STATES OF AMERICA

The McCall Publishing Company
230 Park Avenue, New York, New York 10017

Design by Tere LoPrete

FOREWORD

"Weight goes down when calorie intake goes down and practically everything we eat contains at least some calories."

You will find that sentence near the beginning of this book and it is true. Had I written this book I would have preceded it with this sentence: "Weight goes down when calorie expenditure goes up and every time you use your muscles it uses up calories."

And I would have modified that first sentence by saying, ". . . and practically everything we eat *and drink* (except water, black coffee, and plain tea) contains at least some calories." Placing a sentence on caloric expenditure ahead of caloric intake tends to emphasize what I think is the major factor in causing obesity in most people—lack of physical activity.

But regardless of these differences in our points of view, *Redbook* magazine has done a good job in putting together in convenient book form its Wise Woman's Diet, accompanying it with a series of well-planned menus and a great variety of recipes—and closing with an exercise program.

On the nutritional side of the Wise Woman's Diet, *Redbook* had the help of an outstanding physician-nutritionist, Dr. George Christakis, who had a great deal of firsthand experience in dealing with problems of obesity when he was in charge of the nutrition clinics operated by the Health Department of the City of New York. These outstanding clinics were originated by the late Dr. Norman Jolliffe, another leader in medical nutrition in this country. I know of no other city that has done as good a job as New York in the development of nutrition clinics operated by their health department, and Dr. Christakis deserves much of this credit.

"All of the menus in the Wise Woman's Diet have been devised with particular attention to variety and eating pleasure," this book says and it is a sentence of considerable importance. Variety in foods consumed is the keystone to good nutrition and thus to sensible dieting. There is no single food, not even mother's milk, that contains all the nutrients necessary for the best of health. There is no perfect food, though milk (and here I mean cow's milk) comes the closest to a perfect food. In my opinion, however, the new, 1 percent milks (1 percent fat rather than 3 percent fat or more) with 2 percent extra skim milk solids are a nutritional improvement over whole milk because they have fewer total calories, less saturated fat, and more proteins, calcium, phosphorus, B vitamins, and the other nutrients in the milk solids.

Since no single food by itself provides good nutrition we must consume a variety of foods to get all of the fifty-some known nutrients—amino acids, vitamins, minerals, fatty acids, and the basic sugar, glucose, a constituent of ordinary table sugar (which is sucrose).

In 1955 Harvard's Department of Nutrition devised what we called the Basic 4 Shield of Good Nutrition. This simply divided all of our foods into four groups: the meat, fish, egg, or protein group; the diary group; the vegetable and fruit group; and the cereal group. By consuming each day, and preferably at each meal, one or more foods from each of the Basic 4 food groups, most people are assured of good nutrition—provided they don't consume too many calories, or if they do, they burn (exercise) them up, and provided they live in a community that has had the intelligence and gumption to adjust the fluoride content of its water. For most communities this means the addition of a small amount of the mineral nutrient fluoride to the water, a process known as fluoridation. This is one of the truly great nutritional advances of modern public health.

Variety in food consumption among the Basic 4 food groups is the key to better nutrition, and the menus to implement the Wise Woman's Diet provide good variety from the Basic 4.

"Eating pleasure!" Eating has always been, and always will be, one of the real pleasures of life, just as it is a physiologic and psychologic necessity. The Wise Woman's Diet with its many menus does provide eating pleasure.

The Wise Woman's Exercise Program at the end of the book describes "Nine Body-Shaping Exercises" and some with names that are odd to me, such as, "Thread the Needle," and "The Cat." It also recommends that "for all-around good health you also need some regular vigorous activity. Running, jogging, bicycling, riding, swimming, and tennis will help you to lose weight faster—and will increase your general physical fitness." (And I might say that if you start and continue some of these huffing and puffing activities before you get fat you probably won't get fat.)

One exercise I didn't see emphasized in the Wise Woman's Exercise Program is walking. But it is an easily available exercise, though the walking should be brisk and frequent. And, if you can find a stairway, never use the elevator or escalator for only two or three flights. You will be surprised what just two brisk extra fifteen minute walks *every day* will do for your weight, your circulation, and your general well being.

Exercise is important in calorie control—the only way one has of using up the many calories from food and drink that are so pleasurable.

"Diet fads come and go as predictably as the weight lost and regained on them."

But the Wise Woman's Diet is not a fad. It should become your new way of eating. It is based on good, respected medical nutrition advice. And this is hard to find today.

Redbook's Wise Woman's Diet and Exercise Book is for you.

Fredrick J. Stare, M.D.
Professor of Nutrition
Chairman, Department of Nutrition
Harvard University School of Public Health
Boston, Massachusetts

CONTENTS

———❀❀❀———

INTRODUCTION

❀❀❀

DIET fads come and go as predictably as the weight lost and regained on them. Low-carbohydrate diets, high-fat diets, six-bananas-a-day diets—all are based on the principle of drastically reducing the daily intake of certain nutrients. Because of their nutritional imbalances, crash diets are not intended for long-term use. The dieter eventually abandons a fad diet and returns to her old eating pattern—and her old weight.

The Wise Woman's Diet, first published in *Redbook* three years ago, has outlasted scores of such fad diets. Its varied, nutritionally sound menus have helped thousands of women shed pounds safely and simply. The Wise Woman's Diet can help you take off weight, too, comfortably and without the agonizing hunger pangs that accompany crash or fad diets. Perhaps the best thing about the Wise Woman's Diet is that it helps you to establish good eating habits. And it is primarily such habits that can forestall the frustrating loss and gain of weight that most dieters suffer.

The original Wise Woman's Diet was devised in cooperation with Dr.

George Christakis, former director of the Bureau of Nutrition in the New York City Department of Health and now associate dean and professor of Community Medicine (nutrition) at Mount Sinai School of Medicine in New York City. Devoid of trickery and gimmicks, the diet is based on sound, balanced nutrition, which is the only wise way for anyone to take off weight. (No one, of course, should embark on any diet plan without checking first with her own doctor.) The first Wise Woman's Diet was so enthusiastically received by *Redbook*'s readers, as well as by experts in the field of nutrition, that the magazine developed several series of menus based on the diet. Because it is apparent that the diet is successful—in the first eighteen months of its publication, over 30,000 requests for reprints of it were received—*Redbook* has put the entire collection of menus and recipes together in this book for the convenience of women who wish to use the Wise Woman's Diet for themselves and their families in their daily lives.

The ultimate goal of any diet is not just to get rid of excess weight temporarily but to keep it off permanently. On the following pages we will explain how and why the Wise Woman's Diet can help you reach your ideal weight and maintain it for a lifetime. We will also explain why exercise is an important factor in any realistic reducing regimen. Shedding pounds is, of course, only a part of the total slimming battle. If you are overweight and want a better figure, you should accompany the Wise Woman's Diet with a daily exercise routine. The best way to get rid of excess fat and make muscles firm is to decrease your intake of fattening foods and increase your output of physical energy by exercise. On page 101 you will find a series of nine body-shaping exercises that were originally published in *Redbook* because of their record of success in figure improvement.

The Wise Woman's Diet

The Wise Woman's Diet is a nutritionally sound, 1,200 calories-a-day plan. This amount of calories is not dramatically low, but it is probably about 1,000 calories less than you are eating now. Since approximately 3,500 calories equal one pound of fat, you can lose about a pound every three and one-half days or between two and three pounds a week, depending on how active you are. The diet allows you three good meals a day and more since each of the menus provides supplements in case you feel hungry between meals. Once you have reached your goal and lost as much weight as you planned, you can maintain the lower weight by continuing on the menus but increasing your daily intake by about four hundred calories.

One of the primary reasons for the success of the Wise Woman's Diet is that the entire family can eat and enjoy the menus. Anyone who has ever tried to lose weight knows what attacks of self-pity can be brought on by sitting at the table picking at dreary little bits of food while everyone else digs into the mashed potatoes and gravy. On the Wise Woman's Diet you are not left to a lonely, grimly monotonous special menu—you are able to eat regular family meals, scaled down to prescribed proportions. While the dieter cuts down her food intake to the amounts advised, the rest of the family may have as much as they choose.

A further bonus is that the diet cannot only start you on correct eating habits but can also establish them for your children and prevent them from having overweight problems when they grow up. The great variety of dishes will keep you interested in the foods you eat and help avoid depression and monotony, the pitfalls of so many efforts to lose weight. But more important than taste appeal and enjoyment, the menus provide sound nutrition. The diet allocates about 25 percent of the total daily calories to proteins, 45 percent to carbohydrates, and 30 percent to fats, two-thirds of which are the unsaturated type. When followed as directed, this diet plan is so balanced that no supplementary vitamins or minerals are necessary. All the elements you and your family need for health and energy are right there.

Each of the menus in the Wise Woman's Diet includes six ounces of protein, usually meat, fish, or poultry every day. This actually makes larger portions than it would seem because the amounts represent cooked weight after all bone and other inedible parts have been removed. In order to get four ounces of boneless poultry, for example, you would need to cook half a pound. The amount of fat in raw meat varies so much that definite comparisons cannot be given. On the average, though, six ounces of raw, boneless steak will equal four after broiling; four ounces of ground beef will cook down to three. Fish fillets shrink very little in cooking. Remember, always, to select the leanest pieces of meat when you shop and to remove as much of the visible fat as possible.

To provide all other necessary food elements, a starchy vegetable or pasta, leafy vegetables, fruits, skim milk, bread, cereal, and fat are included. This amount of food may not seem possible on a 1,200-calorie reducing diet, but it is and it works! There is one important rule to remember: *The meals are not interchangeable. Never substitute a meal from one day's menu for another.* To any of the menus you may add black coffee or tea with lemon if desired.

The first series of menus in the Wise Woman's Diet were the result of work by Dr. Christakis and his staff of public health nutritionists in New York City. Over a period of fourteen years some 28,000 patients attended the city's health department clinics in the most massive weight-reducing program ever conducted in this country. The nutritionists discovered that common sense is seldom the factor that makes a diet appeal to an overweight patient. They found, for example, that patients were unwilling to follow the sensible but somehow unexciting diet sheets that many doctors give them. The first set of meal plans, a series of seven international menus, was devised in order to give *balanced* diets the kind of glamour that patients desired in a weight-reducing plan.

The patients who attended the New York City Health Department clinics came from a variety of ethnic backgrounds. New York, one of the most cosmopolitan cities in the world, is comprised of many different national communities in which the eating habits of people vary greatly. Since there are overweight people of every nationality, the nutritionists wanted the diets to appeal to as many of these groups as possible. The international menus on page 29 were designed originally for German, Italian, French, Spanish, Jewish, Russian, and American tastes.

Dr. Christakis pointed out that when, for instance, a housewife of Italian descent gets fat, she gets fat with an Italian accent, so to speak. And when she wants to lose weight, it is easier if her reducing diet can be built around foods she normally prepares for herself and her family. The same is true, of course, for women of other ethnic backgrounds. The diets were planned to take weight off safely with foods familiar to the various groups. For example, an Italian may like carbohydrates in the form of pasta, while a North American may prefer a baked potato, and someone from Puerto Rico might choose rice.

Many of the foreign dishes in the international menus were high in fat in their original forms. They have been adapted to provide low-calorie, low-fat substitutes without losing characteristic flavors. Sour cream, for example, is a basic ingredient of Russian and Jewish cooking, but it has a high-fat content and therefore is high in calories. "Our own brand" of sour

[6]

cream is made by mixing skim milk, cottage cheese, and lemon juice in a blender. The result amounts to only thirty calories when a spoonful garnishes a bowl of borsch or a dish of Beef Stroganoff.

The Italian menus presented greater problems because Italian food usually is rich and fattening. In adapting those menus, traditional flavors were retained by using lemon, garlic, oregano, rosemary, and other herbs containing few or no calories. Canned tomatoes are substituted for thick tomato paste, and, by careful use, one tablespoonful of oil will sauté onions and meat for a main dish to serve four people.

The total calorie content of the menus is further reduced by balancing high-calorie national dishes with low-calorie ones. The French, for example, enjoy mushrooms, artichokes, and endive—all low in calories—as well as filet mignon, which is high. The Germans like sauerkraut, as well as dumplings, and the Italians eat zucchini and also spaghetti.

These menus are an exciting adventure in international cuisine. You will probably find new taste sensations in their preparation you might never have experienced otherwise. Imagine having such mouth-watering dishes as veal and peppers, chicken cacciatore, shrimp con riso, or lamb curry on a diet!

The seven international menus were so successful that the Wise Woman's Diet was expanded by *Redbook*'s home economists to include menus that would appeal to larger sections of the American public. Not everyone, for example, can spend a lot of time in the kitchen. Women who work need menus that can be planned ahead to allow for their preparation. Furthermore, working women must beware of lunch-hour temptations in restaurants. With these readers in mind, the *Redbook* kitchens developed a fourteen-day edition of the Wise Woman's Diet that includes lunches that can be packed to take along to work or eaten at home for five days of each week's menus. This same two-week series also features dishes that are glamorous enough to serve dinner guests and that can be prepared in a limited time outside of working hours.

In addition, there is also a special version of the Wise Woman's Diet that has been planned especially for summer and its many taste treats. In the summertime the living may be easy for many people but not for the woman who is struggling to keep a bathing-suit figure. The season brings with it a full crop of new temptations—picnics and casual meals, tall, cool, sweetened beverages, and a relaxed, vacation atmosphere. The Wise Woman's

Diet for summer slimming is also based on 1,200 calories a day and on the same principle of sound nutrition combined with enjoyable meals. You can lose weight and still enjoy the season's bounty of fresh fruits and vegetables, as well as traditional picnic foods, including sandwiches.

How to Use the Wise Woman's Diet

When you first begin the Wise Woman's Diet, weigh all portions of meat, fish, and poultry if you possibly can. A postage scale covered with foil or plastic wrap will do. You can also buy a special dieter's scale in most large hardware stores. After you have been on the diet for a period of time, you will be able to judge fairly accurately how much the portions weigh by looking at them. Each menu has been carefully planned to equal approximately 1,200 calories a day, which relieves you of the tedious and annoying job of figuring out how many calories each of the various foods contains. However, in order for the diet to work most effectively, you may not exceed the exact amounts recommended and, until you develop an eagle eye through practice, measure everything. Don't guess.

Don't skip a meal. Eat every one of the three in each day's menu at a regular hour. Permanent weight reduction depends on retraining poor eating habits. If you never eat breakfast or if you are one of those self-deceivers who can't understand why you are fat because you only have one meal a day, this diet will soon train you to anticipate and enjoy three wholesome, nutritious meals on a regular basis.

Keep an account of everything you eat, especially at the beginning of the diet. Dieters often develop amazingly convenient memories. A type of patient familiar to doctors the country over is the one who complains, "My husband (or my friend, neighbor, sister) can eat everything in sight and never gain an ounce. It isn't fair. I constantly go without but all I have to do is just look at food and I get fat!" The doctor would probably suggest that she stop looking and start choosing lower calorie, more nutritious foods. This type of dieter may indeed go without a meal all day long and then pack in an enormous dinner, but she won't think of it as fattening and she won't count the calories. She may remember how hungry she felt nibbling on that piece of celery at noon and the dinner is a reward for being a good girl. She may really think she is making a great effort to lose weight, but she will not take into account the two whiskey sours before dinner or the cream in three cups of coffee that morning or the fruit she nibbled in the afternoon.

Weight goes down when calorie intake goes down and practically everything we eat contains at least some calories. Successful weight reduction depends on controlling the *total* number of calories each day. Until you train yourself to censor out extra calories automatically, carry a little notebook with you and jot down every one of the extras you "forgot" and ate that day. Add up the total calories. It may surprise you to see how many they add up to. They could make all the difference in shedding those pounds quickly.

WHAT YOU SHOULD KNOW
IN ORDER TO DIET SUCCESSFULLY

Factors Involved in Overeating and Overweight

The women who decides to lose weight is taking on powerful foes—both within herself and in outside social forces that work to keep her attention focused on food. Magazines, posters, billboards, television, newspapers, and store windows display pictures and advertisements for every conceivable kind of food and drink. Short of living like a hermit, there is no way to avoid these enticements, and the dieter has to make a conscious effort to check herself in the face of all these persuasive pressures.

In addition to cultural and sociological influences, psychological factors almost invariably are present in overeating and overweight. A mound of butter-ripple ice cream can be a fat woman's means of relieving depression and loneliness. She may try to escape the discomfort of tensions, anxieties, and sorrow by stuffing down rich pastries. Or she may overeat to celebrate some happy occasion.

How can you refuse a piece of that beautiful cake your sister baked especially for your birthday party? How can you turn down turkey stuffing and pumpkin pie at your mother's Thanksgiving dinner? What do you do when all your friends and loving relatives urge you to join them at the

[9]

groaning board to celebrate a family gathering or almost any social event when good friends get together? Strong pressures—almost irresistible—and yet you must resist or spend the rest of your life looking like a glob instead of a girl. Considering this, the choice shouldn't be so difficult. Until it finally sinks in that you are determined to stick to your diet, you may stir up a few wounded feelings by refusing fattening goodies. But, if you are truly ready to lose weight, you will be more concerned with getting rid of those pounds than with the temporary emotional reaction of someone else.

People are fat for many different reasons. Some of us eat more than we should because it never occurred to us not to, especially if we come from a part of the country or from a family where large amounts of rich foods are considered important to "the good life." Desserts in particular are often used as expressions of love and affection in such families. When the mother bakes pies, cakes, and cookies, she does so to please her family without ever stopping to think that this may not be the best thing she could do for their health and well-being.

Sweets, for example, are frequently given to children as rewards for good behavior or as love tokens. Such loving gestures are not loving at all. They form a craving for sweets that can burden the child with fat for the rest of her life. There was a time when parents worried about "skinny" children and a fat child was thought to be a healthy child, but research has proven this is not always true. Many overweight children and adults are actually undernourished. Furthermore, a person whose weight problems began in childhood will have a much harder time reducing than one who has put on extra weight in adult life.

Medical research has also brought to light a number of surprising facts in recent years concerning the problem of obesity. Although they are not conclusive at present, some medical studies indicate that the body chemistry of certain people makes them more likely to be fat than others. New evidence has turned up to support the old concept that fat can indeed run in some families. Perhaps the most common misconception about what makes people fat is that it is due to the improper function of the thyroid gland. Here, again, studies show no meaningful difference between thyroid function in people who are obese and those who are not.

Your Motivation for Dieting

People diet for different reasons—some women attempt to reduce in the hope that a slender, youthful body will make their every dream come true. It won't, of course, but that is no reason to be overweight. Sometimes we are goaded into beginning a diet by family pressure and ridicule or in order to compete with other women. The stronger your motivation—or reason for wanting to lose weight—the greater are your chances for success.

Human beings are complicated creatures and candid self-evaluation is nearly always very difficult. Sometimes the truth can—and does—hurt. Nevertheless, if you have put on too many pounds or have always been overweight and want a slender body, you can strengthen your resolve by asking yourself certain questions and answering them as honestly as possible. "Why do I want to lose weight? What made me get into this shape in the first place? Do I really want to get rid of this fat and keep it off forever?"

The more upset you are with the answers, the stronger is your motivation for dieting. Apparently, many of us must reach a point of almost total despair before we are impelled to lose weight and keep it off. If you eat compulsively or if you cannot arrive at understandable answers to the questions, your physician may help you gain insight into the reasons that contribute to your weight problem. Ultimately, your success or failure in dieting depends on how serious you are about losing weight and on understanding and retraining your eating patterns.

Some moderately overweight people can reduce with little more effort than becoming aware of and eliminating from daily menus foods that make them heavier than they want to be. Others react with short tempers, fatigue, or irritation. Many become depressed when deprived of the comfort and security they find in large quantities of rich foods. And some of us just become discouraged by the monotony and give up before reaching our goals.

Doctors are aware of the emotional effects of reducing and frankly admit that controlling obesity is one of the most aggravating problems their profession faces. Most of the trouble is due to the maddening fact that treatment must, of necessity, take a negative rather than a positive direction. "Don't eat thus and so; you may not have that; those foods contain too many calories, stay away from them. . . ." What it amounts to is "No, no, a thousand times, NO!" Small consolation. If you break your arm, a surgeon can set it in a cast until it heals. If you have trouble reading, glasses may be prescribed. When you get an infection, the doctor can give you antibiotics to knock it out. But when you are overweight, except for temporary and sometimes dangerous measures that we will get to presently, only you and you alone can shed the pounds and keep them off.

Calories and Weight Reduction

Regardless of why we are too fat or what motivates us to diet, there are two basic factors that apply to every normal person who wants to lose weight and not gain it back—*ever*. One is a matter of simple mathematics. A calorie is no more than a measurement used to determine the amount of energy (fuel) the body burns up (oxidizes). Calories are burned in proportion to your body's activity. When you eat more calories than you burn up, the excess fuel is stored in fat cells and deposited in various parts of your body. No two bodies store these fat deposits exactly the same. Sometimes they are distributed fairly evenly but more frequently they are concentrated on the thighs, buttocks, backs of the upper arms, or abdomen. Your body will not call on these excess stores unless it needs to burn more calories for energy than you have eaten. When you are active, you use more energy and burn calories at a faster rate. This is why the combination of diet *and* exercise is so vastly more successful, and usually much faster in weight reduction, than diet alone. *The only way to lose fat is to burn more calories than you eat.*

Correcting Eating Habits

The second thing in common we must accept is that eating patterns are learned—practically all eating is habit. If you were raised in a family where heavy, rich foods and sweet desserts were a part of everyday menus, you, naturally, formed a habit for this type of diet. Yet there are many people who do not like sweets and other rich foods. Had you been given a piece of fruit instead of a piece of candy or some carrot sticks instead of cookies when you wanted a snack, and if the rest of your normal diet had consisted of low-calorie, nutritious foods, you would never have developed a taste for things that make you fat. If you had never eaten a wedge of banana cream pie, how could you miss it?

Deeply ingrained habits, admittedly, are hard to break, especially if they were formed in childhood. However, with conscious and determined effort almost any habit can be changed. *The only way to keep weight off once you have lost it is to adjust your permanent eating habits to a lower calorie diet.* It can be done, perhaps more easily than you think. The Wise Woman's Diet will help you get started. The important thing is not to put it off. Start now! Doctors have conducted many experiments concerning human eating patterns, and some have come up with the encouraging conclusion that if you eliminate a certain food from your diet for six months, the desire for it will disappear no matter how much you craved it before. The balanced menus in the Wise Woman's Diet will help you lose weight comfortably and, because they extend over a period of time, will also help you adjust to permanent, lower calorie eating habits.

Why a Diet Should Be Nutritionally Sound

As we mentioned previously, the Wise Woman's Diet allocates about 45 percent to carbohydrate, 25 percent to protein, and 30 percent to fat in the total daily calories. It is important to know why you must maintain a balance between these three vitally necessary elements while cutting down on calories. The American housewife today is better informed about foods and knows more about nutrition than her grandmother ever dreamed of. Vitamins, minerals, proteins, calories, carbohydrates, cholesterol—all are terms with which she is familiar. She may have taken courses in high school or college and learned the importance of a balanced diet for her family's health.

But when she herself decides to lose weight, she may ignore this knowledge. Instead of cutting down in sensible proportion on all three elements, she may try a crash diet or the current popular fad diet that cuts way down on only one of them. As a result, the nutritional imbalance can have various detrimental effects on her health. What is more, it can make keeping to the diet more difficult by robbing her of energy or causing emotional reactions.

Only a few years ago even experts in the field of nutrition thought most weight loss came from fatty tissue. However, recent research has indicated that improperly balanced nutrition can cause weight to be lost from other areas of the body. Proteins, for example, supply vital building blocks for muscle tissue. If the supply of protein is too low during the weight reduction process when it is needed the most, your body starts taking it from muscles. Unfortunately, dieters will not be warned by any physical symptoms when the loss of muscle tissue begins. At one time a popular diet consisted of six bananas and a quart of skim milk a day. Ordinarily a time limit was set on this diet, and it was thought to be harmless even if weight lost was quickly regained when the dieter returned to her former eating habits. But recent studies show that people can suffer harmful metabolic results from such a low protein diet in as few as six days.

There are highly complicated links between carbohydrate and protein metabolism that can best be understood by nutrition experts and the medical profession. A simplified explanation that will serve our purpose here is that enough carbohydrate must be included so that the body need not produce it from its tissue protein, and enough protein so that the body does not lose its lean muscle mass during a period of weight reduction. Adequate carbohydrates are needed for ready energy and for the vitamins contained in many high carbohydrate foods such as the B vitamins from cereals and vitamins A and C from fruits and vegetables.

In addition, when the diet is low in carbohydrates, it almost has to be high in fat. Saturated fats found in butter and ice cream, for example, raise the cholesterol level of the blood, whereas margarines and most liquid vegetable oils drive it down. If too much saturated fat is eaten over a sustained period of time, the resulting high level of cholesterol in the blood increases the risk of heart attack. Another undesirable effect is that acidosis can result when the body burns too much fat.

These are only a few of the reasons why carefully balanced meals such as those in the Wise Woman's Diet are necessary. Even the brain, which depends almost solely on the blood's sugar supply for its energy needs, and other organs as well, can be deprived of important sources of energy by improper diet. The symptoms resulting from this deprivation can be fatigue, irritation, or depression, and they may discourage the dieter to the point where she returns to her old eating patterns in despair.

Crash and Fad Diets and Other Magic

When it comes to dieting, people in a hurry to shed pounds cast caution to the winds. No matter how ridiculous it may be, we will try anything that promises to be the magic formula. We try hundreds of crash and fad diets hoping to lose weight practically overnight and with almost no effort on our part. These diets may work, too, at least for a while. Pounds vanish, we revel in the lift to our spirits and the pride of achievement that a slimmer, new look gives us, only to find, sooner or later, that somehow almost every miserable ounce has crept back on and we are right back to our same old fat selves. So the vicious cycle must be repeated and each time losing weight is harder than it was before.

Diet Pills

Instead of accepting the obvious truth that, ultimately, only willpower and determination can keep anyone away from the refrigerator door, many people want to believe that pills will make fat disappear like magic with no effort on their part. It is true that doctors can—and frequently do—prescribe diet pills for some of their patients. Sometimes pills will help people who might otherwise not be able to summon up the necessary willpower to get started on diets. In such instances the prescription serves a valid and sensible purpose but only under careful medical supervision and only for a limited time. The state of some patients' health, however, makes it highly dangerous for them to take diet pills.

Have a Physical Checkup Before Starting on Any Diet

Knowing you are in good health will contribute to your peace of mind. If there is any reason why you should not diet, your doctor can explain it to you and perhaps prescribe some weight-reducing program to be carried out under his supervision. An overweight person can have problems of which she is unaware, conditions such as high blood pressure, diabetes, or heart disease, which are sometimes associated with obesity. Certainly no one should ever take any kind of reducing pills without being under a doctor's care and unless he prescribes them for her alone. To ignore this rule can be extremely dangerous.

Reducing pills generally contain either amphetamines, which act as appetite depressants, or diuretics, which increase bodily secretions including the flow of urine. When you take diuretics, you may be overjoyed to stand on the scales and see how much weight you have dropped. Your triumph will be a hollow one, because the weight lost simply means your body is not retaining as much water as it normally would and the fat—your real enemy—is still there. Obviously this weight will be regained almost overnight once the diuretic pills are discontinued.

It is generally agreed that drugs in the amphetamine group somehow depress the appetite by speeding up the rate of metabolism. When this process accelerates, our bodies burn calories faster. Amphetamines are addictive drugs that cease to be effective appetite depressants as the body adjusts to tolerate them, usually in about six weeks. Their danger results from a need or desire to increase the daily amount. They can also cause such side reactions as insomnia, irritability, sweating, restlessness, tenseness, and dry mouth. Amphetamines, at best, are a temporary crutch to lean on and, even if you could easily stop taking them, you would not have dealt with the problem that caused you to become fat in the first place.

"Only Fifteen Pounds"

One of the greatest and least referred to obstacles a fat person must overcome is admitting to herself that she is overweight in the first place. A fat woman applying makeup before a mirror prefers to think of her face as "round" or "pleasingly plump" even if it looks like a full moon. If she has two or three chins instead of one, she simply won't look at them. She may habitually wear dark clothes believing she looks smaller in them than in bright colors. Which she may, but not *that* much smaller. Fat women who will readily admit they may be "a little plump" or that they ought to "lose a few pounds" often delude themselves about just how much overweight they really are.

When you hear a five-foot, two-inch tall, size eighteen wistfully sighing something like, "If I could only lose fifteen pounds, I would look great," *you* know by looking at her that this is fantasy. But *she* either cannot or will not admit it to herself. If she has always been fat, she may not have a real conception of how much she should lose or how much more attractive she would be with a slender body. If she used to be slender, admitting to herself that she has eaten her way up from a size ten can be too painful. It is easier for her to believe that losing fifteen pounds rather than fifty pounds will turn her into an attractive woman.

Instructors in some weight-reducing programs approve of this form of self-deception. They reason that some very overweight people are addicted to eating in the same way some alcoholics are addicted to drinking. If giving up food is made to seem too great an effort for these people, they become discouraged and revert back to those impulsive refrigerator raids. But, if a fat woman is encouraged to start dieting by believing her goal should be a weight loss of fifteen pounds instead of fifty, she is more likely to stick to the diet. When she is fifteen pounds lighter and starts taking in her clothes, she begins to realize how marvelous it would be to get down to a size twelve or ten. Her self-esteem rises, the goal is worth reaching, and achieving it no longer seems impossible.

Regulating Your Food Intake

This may surprise you. Taking off those last thirty-five pounds can be easier than losing the first fifteen. The hypothalamus gland regulates our feelings of hunger and satiety, but we do not all feel hunger and satisfy it in the same way or at the same intervals of time. A balanced, nutritious diet eaten at regular intervals helps put the brakes on your hypothalamus. The longer you stay on the diet, the easier it will be for you to feel satisfied with less food. We often hear people who have started to diet say, "I'm hungry. I'm going to feel hungry until my stomach shrinks." A stomach packed full of food, naturally, is going to distend, but when it empties out, it will revert back to normal size. What many people think of as shrinking is in fact the result of diminished demands of the hypothalamus.

Eating habits are changed impulse by impulse. Let's say, for example, you have recently started the Wise Woman's Diet and are feeling rather proud of yourself for eating exactly what it allows and not a half an ounce more. You are probably pleasantly surprised to discover that you are not nearly as hungry as you thought you might be. The telephone rings and you hear some upsetting news. Your first reaction is to put down the phone, grab your coat, and head like a homing pigeon for comfort in the form of a strawberry sundae at the local ice-cream parlor. Try not to obey that impulse, and don't go off the diet. In a short time the impulse will pass and each time you survive one of these crises, you will build more strength to resist the next. If, in spite of all good intentions, you do slip up, get back on the diet with the next meal on that day's menu at your regular time.

EXERCISE: FOR FIGURE IMPROVEMENT
AND FOR LASTING HEALTH AND FITNESS

WE Americans live in the largest, most prosperous, most technically advanced nation that has ever existed in history. Our scientists are transplanting vital organs to prolong life and using other techniques and innovations so advanced they would have seemed like science fiction only a short time ago. We have the best sanitation in the world. We have more research laboratories, technical equipment, electronic inventions, and appliances than could ever be counted. We produce and consume a greater variety and abundance of food than any country on earth.

With all of this going for us it seems logical that we would be healthier, stronger, generally more physically fit, and live longer than any other nation. But something insidious is happening. After years at or near the top in life expectancy, the United States now ranks far behind many countries. And we are not the men and women our forebears were, either. All the hard work they had to put out in order to survive gave them stronger hearts, leaner muscles, and greater physical stamina. True, they were easy prey for the great infectious diseases but today medical science has all but eliminated these killers, and we still are not as physically fit as they were— far from it. The very abundance and easy life we enjoy have created a paradox that is turning more and more Americans into old-young adults.

Our affluent society has created a national health hazard. As our food supplies grow in luxury and variety, our work grows more sedentary. Mention the word "exercise" and most Americans will react as though you have said something distasteful. Except for competitive sports we, as a nation, despise any kind of formal exercise. As a consequence our bodies are deteriorating faster, far too many of us are fatter than we should be, and the risk of heart attacks is increasing. American children are taller and heavier than those of most other nations but tests for strength, endurance, and agility show they have less stamina and are weaker in muscle power than the children in some other countries where the general standard of living is lower than ours.

Whether or not we are aware of it, all of us in the United States are bombarded with pressures and persuasions that tend to keep us tucking into foods that make us fat but not necessarily fit or healthy. Television viewing is our national pastime. It keeps the family together and the children off the streets. It also keeps us fat and flabby. What is cozier than settling down for the family's favorite TV show, especially after a nice, big dinner? Good, wholesome entertainment—and while we are sitting there glued to the tube scarcely a muscle twitches. And certainly no one was hungry when the program began but, suddenly, there flashes on the screen a casserole of the most mouth-watering noodles, or a luscious cake with inch-high frosting, or the coolest, frothiest glass of beer—all accompanied by a masterful sales pitch of friendly persuasion.

Somewhere in your brain the hunger reflex is triggered; the message has gotten through. You may not rush to the kitchen and whip up a seven-layer cake, but you will probably find yourself dashing out during the next commercial for snacks to munch on during the remainder of the program— something fattening, no doubt, unless you are wise enough to keep on hand the crisp vegetable tray included in your diet. You can carry the fattening snacks around on your hips forever. When the late show is over, do you yawn, get up from your comfortable chair, and launch into an exercise routine? Exercise! At midnight? Of course not! Your body never has a chance to burn off the calories in those snacks or in that good dinner.

[19]

What Is Exercise?

Actually, whenever you use any muscle in your body, it is a form of exercise and means that you are converting calories into energy. Specifically planned exercises will improve body proportions and firm up certain muscles more than others. And these needn't be torturous sessions that leave you aching with pain. An easy-paced, body-shaping program faithfully adhered to for a short time every day will do more for your figure than trying to correct body faults quickly with sporadic, violent activity. Hit-and-miss exercising can be painful, discouraging, and, in the long run, dangerous.

There's scarcely a woman in sight who couldn't use a few shape-ups. Even those of us who were lucky enough to be blessed with lithe, slender figures can wake up one morning and notice a sneaky little sag or bulge here and there; after the new baby, perhaps, or because we had settled into comfortable domesticity and hadn't been taking much notice. If nature was generous enough to give you a beautiful body, you certainly owe it to yourself to keep it in shape. If she wasn't, a body-shaping program (especially combined with diet if you are overweight) can do wonders to correct figure faults. And it is never too late to begin. Naturally, if you have been sitting around virtually motionless most of your life, you wouldn't leap into an Olympic champion's workout. You wouldn't be able to if you tried. But when you exercise sensibly and regularly, your body will respond to what you ask of it. Lasting figure-shaping results come from being a tortoise— not a hare.

The Wise Woman's Exercise Program

The special shape-up program beginning on page 101 is planned to concentrate on areas where the body usually stores its largest fat deposits; especially hips, thighs, buttocks, waistline, and abdomen. Some of these exercises are particularly beneficial as muscle toners for new mothers eager to regain their figures. The nine exercises included here were selected from special programs devised for *Redbook* readers. They have a record of success not only because they are pleasant and easy to do but also because they work.

Professional instructors advise starting first with light, rhythmic exercises for several minutes to warm up the body gradually. This prepares the muscles for more strenuous activity by increasing circulation and raising body temperature. Begin with such simple movements as stretching your arms up over your head, flopping the upper part of your body down from the waist in rag-doll fashion, doing half knee bends and arm swings.

Concentrate on each of the exercises in the routine and perform each movement accurately. Music is a pleasant accompaniment and can help you establish a more rhythmic precision. Repeat each exercise sequence ten times, then concentrate on one or two earmarked for your particular figure problems. Taper off gradually at the end of each session, breathing slowly and deeply from the diaphragm. Stretching out flat on the floor while you do this can give you a marvelously relaxed feeling.

Common sense should tell you not to expect results overnight. After six weeks of daily exercises, you should see pleasing contour changes, and from then on you will see more and more. And here is a thought to get you moving. The heavier you are, the faster you get results. A woman who weighs 160 pounds, for example, has to use more energy in even mild exercise than a woman who weighs 125 pounds. The effort required to move around those extra 35 pounds burns calories faster.

You will make a stronger habit of the routine and take it more seriously if you can arrange to do it around the same time every day. The time of day—whether morning, afternoon, or evening—is not important, but forming the habit is. The only time *not* suitable for exercising is immediately after eating. Wait about an hour to start after your largest meal of the day or less time if you have eaten lightly. In order to get meaningful results, the absolute minimum time spent doing the exercises should be ten minutes, beginners included. As you continue in the routine and your muscles strengthen, you may want to speed up your figure improvement by exercising longer.

Wearing tights and a leotard as professionals do is helpful because this costume permits freedom of movement and clearly reveals your body outline, which allows you to judge your progress by observing changes in your proportions. Otherwise, a bathing suit or shorts or slacks and a top will serve the purpose as long as the clothing is comfortable and lets you move without constriction.

The Benefits of Exercise

These nine exercises will make you more limber and help correct contours, but for all-around physical fitness you need some kind of regular, vigorous activity. Much of our tin-ear apathy in this country results from not understanding what exercise is or the tremendous and varied benefits we can reap from it. Consider the many activities you think of as fun rather than exercise. Dancing is one. And don't laugh; more than one football coach includes waltzing in the team's training program. Try waltzing with all the dips and flourishes for fifteen minutes and you will understand why, if you last that long. Bicycling, swimming (considered the most nearly perfect exercise), jogging, hiking, table tennis, skating, and even brisk walking are all enjoyable activities that will firm up muscles to one degree or another, increase your physical fitness, and help you lose weight faster when combined with dieting.

Exercise can keep you from being hungry. Let's say you are one of the thousands of people who shudder at the mention of the word exercise. But you are overweight so you diet to slim down because you want a better figure. You keep faithfully to the diet but otherwise continue in your usual placid, inactive life. You don't ask your body to burn calories faster; you simply give it fewer to burn. If your rate of metabolism is low, your body will function on so few calories that you cannot ever eat enough to really feel satisfied. You are then faced with the choice of going forever hungry or burning calories faster. Under these circumstances some form of daily exercise can be an absolute pleasure.

Exercise will keep you looking and feeling younger, longer. When the cells in your body are not properly nourished, they age and die. Their nourishment depends on good circulation which, in turn, results from keeping your body active. The more you exercise, the better your circulation will be. It also makes you less sensitive to heat and cold.

Exercise will develop your lung capacity. You can do more with less breath and recover more quickly from fatigue. It will increase your vitality and diminish tensions and anxieties. Remember how soundly you used to sleep after playing hard when you were a child? Hard play is hard exercise.

Increased physical activity helps create a sense of well-being and an impression on others of being younger than your actual age. If your main exercise in life has consisted of piling on weight with a knife and fork at the dinner table, you have never formed your own personal image of being a slim, attractive, and vital woman. Somewhere in there is a new, vigorous you, and she is worth all the effort it takes to bring her out. Tighten up those lax muscles and shed those extra pounds with a schedule of regular diet and exercise, and your low opinion of yourself can change to one of healthy self-esteem.

It takes no more self-discipline to stay on a reducing diet with exercise than without it. Quite the opposite. Because regular exercise combined with diet shapes up figures so much faster, it can increase your determination to stick to the diet.

Your Ideal Weight

What is your ideal weight? It should be when you look your best and feel your most energetic. Here, again, if you have always been fat, you have no way of knowing how much better you could look and feel as a slender woman. Doctors today use charts compiled by insurance companies to arrive at the most desirable weight for a patient according to her height and body structure. Formerly these charts were based on average weights, but, because so many of us were too fat in the first place, the weights were not our most desirable because they were too heavy. Today's chart (see page 24) is based on actuarial life and death figures and reflects lower, healthier weights.

To find your most desirable weight, measure your exact height, then examine yourself objectively to determine if your body frame is small, medium, or large. Broad shoulders, a wide pelvis, thick wrists, large hands and feet are indications of a large frame. The opposite indicates a small frame. If your frame is large, naturally you will weigh more because large bones are heavier than small ones. Try to be realistic in assessing your bone structure. The charts vary as much as 30 pounds between desirable weights for the smallest frame and the largest for persons of the same height. If you

[23]

DESIRABLE WEIGHTS FOR WOMEN AGE 25 AND OVER*

HEIGHT (with shoes on — 2-inch heels)		WEIGHT IN POUNDS ACCORDING TO FRAME (in Indoor Clothing)		
FEET	INCHES	SMALL FRAME	MEDIUM FRAME	LARGE FRAME
4	10	92 — 98	96 — 107	104 — 119
4	11	94 — 101	98 — 110	106 — 122
5	0	96 — 104	101 — 113	109 — 125
5	1	99 — 107	104 — 116	112 — 128
5	2	102 — 110	107 — 119	115 — 131
5	3	105 — 113	110 — 122	118 — 134
5	4	108 — 116	113 — 126	121 — 138
5	5	111 — 119	116 — 130	125 — 142
5	6	114 — 123	120 — 135	129 — 146
5	7	118 — 127	124 — 139	133 — 150
5	8	122 — 131	128 — 143	137 — 154
5	9	126 — 135	132 — 147	141 — 158
5	10	130 — 140	136 — 151	145 — 163
5	11	134 — 144	140 — 155	149 — 168
6	0	138 — 148	144 — 159	153 — 173

For girls between 18 and 25, subtract 1 pound for each year under 25.

* *Data prepared by the Metropolitan Life Insurance Company*

have a petite bone structure and deceive yourself into believing it is large, the difference means that you are carrying around those extra pounds as fat. Some people with small frames will weigh more than the charts indicate if they have built up large, heavy muscles. However, since most fat people are known to shun exercise, large muscles will seldom account for their extra weight.

A reasonably accurate measurement of how fat you are can be made by a simple pinch test on the back of your upper arm. Flex your right arm at a ninety-degree angle and pinch a full fold of back skin firmly between your thumb and forefinger exactly halfway between your elbow and shoulder. Hold onto it and let your arm drop and hang loosely. Pull the thickness of skin out from the underlying tissue. If you are between the ages of eighteen and fifty and maintain your most desirable weight, this double skinfold should measure no more than one-inch in thickness regardless of your age or bone structure. Doctors have found this simple test indicative of the overall fat deposits in the rest of your body regardless of fat patterning. Women—even those of desirable weight—have more fat on their bodies than men. It accounts for the alluring curves we try so hard to keep under control. This measurement applies to women only. The measurement for a man of desirable weight would be much less because he would not have a layer of fat on the upper arm.

Age does not count as far as desirable weight is concerned. Once your body has reached full growth it requires no more calories than those in a well-balanced, nutritious diet that will maintain your most desirable weight throughout adult life. Plump grandmotherly types bulge out in the wrong places because they eat too much, not because they have reached a grand-motherly age.

In present-day America we certainly are not ignorant of the principles of diet and exercise. Overweight and its effects on our appearance and health are subjects of intense interest about which thousands of us are very well informed. Even so, we still hope for magic, for some painless, easy way to shrink off excess fat without getting down to the difficult business of retraining poor eating habits. Reducing, just as many other tasks in life, is not easy to do, and it is made more difficult by deep emotional involvement with pleasures of the palate stemming from childhood. Maintaining weight loss is a matter of changing eating patterns—not just for the duration of a diet, but for a lifetime.

Here are some suggestions from medical specialists and successful women dieters that can help you lose weight and maintain your new, slender figure.

* *Eat each of your meals at the same time every day.* A regular schedule helps you break poor eating habits and form good ones.
* *Never skip a meal.* You need all the meals in the Wise Woman's Diet for balanced nutrition and to help burn off fat. If you should skip one, get back on the diet with the next meal at your usual time.
* *Eat slowly and sit down for meals.* Different people experience satiety at different levels. Eating slowly may help you feel satisfied with less food. More than 90 percent of overweight people are fast and frequently stand-up eaters. Set your table attractively and enjoy a leisurely meal even if you are alone.

[25]

* *Watch those late evening snacks.* If you usually get hungry in the evening, save the daily supplements allowed in the Wise Woman's Diet for this time of temptation or keep on hand fresh vegetables such as carrot sticks, celery, radishes, or cucumbers for nibbling.

* *Never go marketing when you are hungry.* Prepare your complete marketing list before leaving home and shop as soon as possible after a meal. Temptation lurks in food stores so get in and get out fast. When you feel hungry, chew sugarless gum.

* *Carry a "before" picture of yourself in your wallet.* Take a good look at it every time you are tempted to break the diet with something fattening.

* *Don't weigh yourself every day.* Keep an accurate record of your progress but only get on the scales once or twice a week. Weigh yourself at the same hour in the *morning* before breakfast and without clothing.

* *Do some exercise every day.* Even mild exercise is better than none. Stick to an exercise routine even if you think it's going to kill you. It won't. It will become easier, and the fat will disappear faster.

* *Join a mutual-help group or form one of your own.* If going it alone is too hard, investigate a mutual-help group. You may have several friends or neighbors who want to use the Wise Woman's Diet. Get together for moral support; call one another for encouragement when the prospect of an eating binge looms up. Have them call you, and talk them into staying on the diet; you will strengthen your own determination at the same time. Make sure that everyone in the group has a physical checkup first and at least periodical professional supervision.

* *Daydream.* Think of yourself in a perfectly fitting dress two sizes smaller than your present size. Give yourself treats that have nothing to do with food, a different hair style, a new piece of jewelry, whatever will raise your morale until your goal is reached. Good luck!

THE
WISE WOMAN'S
DIET

International Menus and Recipes

❁ ❁ ❁

THE first series of meal plans in the Wise Woman's Diet can be enjoyed by dieters of many nationalities. Developed originally to meet a wide variety of taste preferences—Italian, French, Spanish, Russian, German, and Jewish, as well as American—these menus are truly an adventure in international cuisine. All the recipes have been tested in *Redbook*'s kitchens, so successful results are guaranteed. Although the recipes are simple enough for the average cook to follow, they have the air of gourmet dining usually associated with foreign dishes.

All the menus in the Wise Woman's Diet have been devised with particular attention to variety and eating pleasure. The great advantage of this safe and sensible diet plan is that the whole family can enjoy the meals. Only the dieter need observe the serving quantities specified for staying close to the 1,200-calorie limit recommended for a day. While the dieter limits her portions to the amounts advised, the rest of the family can come back for seconds if they choose.

The menus have been planned carefully to provide a balanced, nutritious diet. However, the meals are not interchangeable; you should not attempt to substitute a meal from one day's menu for another.

Top-of-range temperatures given in *Redbook*'s kitchen-tested recipes are intended for use with thermostatically controlled burners or units and with electric frying pans or griddles. If you use neither, follow the heat requirements described by the words preceding the temperatures.

You may add black coffee or tea with lemon to any of the menus in the Wise Woman's Diet.

Italian Diet
Menu 1 / 1,208 Calories

BREAKFAST

½ cup orange juice
1 cooked egg
1 slice enriched white bread

LUNCH

Antipasto: 1 leaf lettuce
1 celery stalk, 2 radishes, 3 ounces
tuna, and 1 stalk fennel
2 slices Italian bread
½ cup unsweetened fresh
pineapple

DINNER

*Spaghetti and Meat Balls
½ cup broccoli
4 leaves romaine lettuce
1 tablespoon bottled low-calorie
French dressing
1 apple

SUPPLEMENTS

2 cups skim milk
1 pear

* Recipe given

Spaghetti and Meat Balls

1 tablespoon instant minced onion
1 tablespoon water
1 pound ground lean beef
1 small clove garlic, minced
1 tablespoon chopped parsley

1 egg, slightly beaten
¼ teaspoon salt
Few grains pepper
1 tablespoon vegetable oil
Tomato Sauce (recipe below)
Cooked spaghetti

Sprinkle onion over water and let stand 5 minutes to hydrate. Mix meat, onion, garlic, parsley, egg, salt, and pepper together. Shape heaping tablespoons of meat into balls. There should be about 15 balls. Heat oil in skillet over moderately high heat (about 300° F.); brown meat balls on all sides. Add meat balls to hot Tomato Sauce (*recipe below*) and heat over moderately low heat (about 225° F.) 15 minutes. Serve over spaghetti. For diet serving allow 3 meat balls, ½ cup sauce, and ½ cup cooked spaghetti (341 calories). Serves 4.

Tomato Sauce

1 tablespoon vegetable oil	2 tablespoons chopped parsley
1 medium-sized onion, chopped	¾ teaspoon dried oregano leaves
1 clove garlic, minced	½ teaspoon salt
1 1-pound-12-ounce can tomatoes	⅛ teaspoon pepper
1 bay leaf	

Heat oil in skillet over moderate heat (about 250° F.); add onion and garlic and cook until tender. Add tomatoes, bay leaf, parsley, oregano, salt, and pepper; cover and cook over low heat (about 200° F.) 1 hour, stirring occasionally. Makes 3 cups sauce.

Italian Diet
Menu 2 / 1,181 Calories

BREAKFAST

½ grapefruit
½ cup cooked corn meal
1 cup skim milk
2 slices crisp bacon

LUNCH

4 ounces ricotta cheese
½ cup eggplant and 1 cup tomatoes, cooked together
2 slices Italian bread
4 unsweetened cooked prunes

DINNER

1 cup chicken bouillon
*Chicken Cacciatore
1 small baked potato
½ cup cooked zucchini
15 inner chicory leaves
1 tablespoon bottled low-calorie Italian dressing
½ cup water-packed apricot halves

SUPPLEMENTS

2 cups skim milk
1 small banana

* Recipe given

[31]

Chicken Cacciatore

1 3-pound broiler–fryer chicken, cut up
Salt and pepper
1 tablespoon vegetable oil
1 cup canned tomatoes
1 medium-sized green pepper, seeded and sliced
2 medium-sized onions, sliced
1 clove garlic, minced
¾ teaspoon salt
Few grains pepper
1 cup sliced mushrooms

Sprinkle chicken with salt and pepper. Heat oil in skillet over moderately high heat (about 275° F.). Add chicken and cook until lightly browned. Mix tomatoes, green pepper, onion, garlic, the ¾ teaspoon salt, and pepper; pour over chicken, cover and cook over low heat (about 200° F.) 40 minutes. Add mushrooms; cover and cook 20 minutes longer, or until chicken is fork-tender. For diet serving allow 3 ounces of chicken and ¼ of the sauce (161 calories). Serves 4.

Italian Diet
Menu 3 / 1,218 Calories

BREAKFAST

1 orange, sliced
½ cup cooked farina
1 cup skim milk

LUNCH

3 ounces prosciutto (Italian ham)
½ cup melon balls
2 leaves lettuce
2 slices Italian bread

DINNER

*Spinach Soup
*Shrimp Con Riso
6 cooked asparagus spears
1 cup mixed green salad
1 tablespoon bottled low-calorie French dressing
1 pear

SUPPLEMENTS

1 cup skim milk
1 dried fig
1 apple

* Recipe given

Spinach Soup

2 cups finely chopped raw spinach	½ teaspoon salt
⅔ cup diced carrot	Few grains pepper
6 chopped scallions	Parmesan cheese
6 cups canned chicken broth	(optional)

Place all ingredients in a saucepan; bring to a boil and cook over moderate heat (about 250° F.) for 30 minutes, stirring occasionally. If desired, serve with grated Parmesan cheese. For diet serving allow 1 cup (51 calories). Serves 4 to 6.

Shrimp Con Riso

1½ pounds shrimp	2 cups canned tomatoes
Boiling salted water	½ teaspoon dried basil leaves
1 tablespoon vegetable oil	
⅓ cup thinly sliced onion	½ teaspoon salt
½ cup diced celery	Few grains pepper
	2½ cups hot cooked rice

Cook shrimp in salted water over low heat (about 200°F.) for about 5 minutes, or until pink. Do not boil. Heat oil in saucepan over moderate heat (about 250° F.); add onion and celery and cook until tender, stirring occasionally. Add tomatoes, basil, salt, and pepper; cook over low heat (about 200° F.) for 20 minutes, stirring occasionally. Add shrimp, cover and heat for 5 minutes. Serve over the rice. For diet serving allow 3 ounces shrimp, ½ cup sauce, and ⅛ cup rice (166 calories). Serves 4.

Italian Diet
Menu 4 / 1,223 Calories

BREAKFAST

½ cup grapefruit juice
1 ounce dried cereal
1 cup skim milk

LUNCH

*Boiled Whiting
1 pimiento
10 leaves escarole
1 tablespoon bottled low-calorie
French dressing
2 slices Italian bread
⅓ cup water-packed canned plums

* Recipe given

[33]

*Veal and Peppers
½ cup cooked noodles
1 cup raw spinach salad
1 tablespoon bottled low-calorie
French dressing
Citrus cup (½ orange and
½ grapefruit)

1 cup skim milk

* Recipe given

Boiled Whiting

1½ pounds whiting or halibut	1 sprig parsley
1½ teaspoons salt	½ medium-sized onion,
2 cups water	sliced
3 peppercorns	1 bay leaf
½ clove garlic	

Cut fish into serving-size pieces and sprinkle well with salt. Place in a saucepan; add water and remaining ingredients. Bring to a boil; cover and simmer gently over low heat (about 200° F.) 15 to 20 minutes, or until fish is easily flaked with a fork. Do not boil. For diet serving allow 3 ounces fish (135 calories). Serves 4 to 6.

Veal and Peppers

4 medium-sized green peppers	1 pound veal, cut into 1-inch cubes
1 tablespoon vegetable oil	2 cups canned tomatoes
1 medium-sized onion, sliced	1 teaspoon salt
1 tablespoon vegetable oil	Few grains pepper
	6 tablespoons dry white wine

Wash, stem, and seed green peppers; cut each into six sections. Heat the 1 tablespoon oil in skillet over moderate heat (about 250° F.); add onion and green pepper and cook until tender, stirring frequently. Remove onion and green pepper. Add and heat the remaining 1 tablespoon oil; add veal and cook until lightly browned, stirring occasionally. Add tomatoes, salt, and pepper; cover and cook over low heat (about 200° F.) 30 minutes. Add green pepper, onion, and wine; cover and cook 30 minutes longer. For diet serving allow 3 ounces veal and ¼ of the vegetable mixture (337 calories). Serves 4.

BREAKFAST

1 cup coffee with 4 ounces skim milk
1 ounce French bread

LUNCH

Hors d'oeuvres (1 sardine, 1 small artichoke, ¼ tomato, 1 teaspoon oil, and 1 teaspoon vinegar)
3 ounces roast veal
½ cup cooked spinach
1 ounce French bread
½ cup water-packed pineapple chunks

AFTERNOON

1 cup coffee with 4 ounces skim milk

DINNER

*Water-Cress-and-Potato Soup
*Poached Fillet of Sole
½ cup fresh peas cooked with ½ cup Boston lettuce
1 ounce French bread
⅔ cup water-packed sliced peaches in 2 ounces red wine

SUPPLEMENT

1 orange

* Recipe given

Water-Cress-and-Potato Soup   1556585

1 quart canned chicken broth	1 cup coarsely chopped water cress
2 medium-sized potatoes, diced	Salt and pepper
	1 cup hot skim milk

Heat broth over moderately low heat (about 225° F.); add potatoes and water cress, cover and cook about 45 minutes, or until tender. Mash through a strainer or a food mill. Season with salt and pepper. Add milk; heat to serving temperature and serve. For diet serving allow 1 cup (94 calories). Serves 4.

Poached Fillet of Sole

1½ cups water	1 tablespoon vinegar
½ medium-sized onion, sliced	3 peppercorns
1 bay leaf	1 teaspoon salt
1 tablespoon lemon juice	1 pound fillet of sole
	Chopped parsley

Place water, onion, bay leaf, lemon juice, vinegar, peppercorns, and salt in a saucepan and cook over moderate heat (about 250° F.) for 5 minutes.

Cut fish into serving-size pieces and add to the water. Cook over low heat (about 200° F.) 5 to 10 minutes, or until fish is easily flaked with a fork. Sprinkle fish with chopped parsley before serving. For diet serving allow 3 ounces of fish (153 calories). Serves 4.

Spanish Diet / 1,216 Calories

BREAKFAST
Coffee with 6 ounces skim milk
2 ounces Spanish bread
1 orange

LUNCH
*Puchero a la Madrileña
1 small banana
Coffee with 6 ounces skim milk

DINNER
*Fish Soup
2 lettuce leaves
⅛ tomato
1 slice white bread
½ cup sliced water-packed peaches
Coffee with 6 ounces skim milk

SUPPLEMENTS
1 cup skim milk
1 apple

* Recipe given

Puchero a la Madrilena

½ pound lean beef, cubed
1 pound chicken, cut into serving-size pieces
Salt and pepper
1 tablespoon vegetable oil
1½ tablespoons tomato sauce
2 medium-sized onions, chopped
2 cloves garlic, minced

1 cup canned chick peas, drained
4 small potatoes, peeled
2 cups canned tomatoes
1 pound cabbage, cored and cut into wedges
2 teaspoons salt
⅛ teaspoon pepper
Boiling water

Sprinkle beef and chicken with salt and pepper. Heat oil in skillet over moderately high heat (about 300° F.); add beef and chicken and brown on all sides. Remove meat and add tomato sauce; add onion and garlic and cook over moderate heat (about 250° F.) until tender. Return meat to pan; add chick peas, potatoes, tomato, cabbage, the 2 teaspoons salt, and the ⅛ teaspoon pepper. Add some of the liquid from the chick peas and enough boiling water to cover meat and vegetables. Cover and cook over low heat (about 200° F.) 1½ to 2 hours, or until meat is tender. For diet serving allow 2 ounces beef, 2 ounces chicken, and ¼ of the vegetable mixture (374 calories). Serves 4.

Fish Soup

1 medium-sized onion, sliced	Few grains pepper
1 cup canned tomatoes	1 tablespoon vegetable oil
1 carrot, sliced	4 cups water
1 tablespoon chopped parsley	1 pound fish (cod or haddock), cut into serving-size pieces
½ clove garlic, minced	1 vegetable bouillon cube
1½ teaspoons salt	¼ cup rice

Place onion, tomatoes, carrot, parsley, garlic, salt, pepper, oil, and water in a saucepan; bring to a boil and simmer over moderate heat (about 250° F.) until onion is tender. Add fish; cover and cook over low heat (about 200° F.) 5 to 10 minutes, or until fish is easily flaked. Remove fish from soup; add bouillon cube and rice and cook over moderately low heat (about 225° F.) until rice is tender. Return fish to soup and heat before serving. For diet serving allow 4 ounces of fish and ¼ of the vegetables and rice (183 calories). Serves 4.

Russian Diet / 1,215 Calories

BREAKFAST

Hard roll
3 ounces pot cheese

DINNER

*Beef Borsch
Vegetable relish plate:
4 radishes, 6 slices cucumber,
and 2 scallions
1 slice Russian pumpernickel
bread
1 orange, sliced

LUNCH OR SUPPER

3 ounces smoked carp
1 boiled potato
½ sour pickle
Vegetable relish plate: 4 carrot
sticks, ½ sliced tomato, 3 green
pepper slices
½ cup fruit compote (pineapple,
banana, grapes, and orange)

SUPPLEMENTS

1 cup skim milk
1 apple

* Recipe given

[37]

Beef Borsch

1 quart canned beef broth or water
1 leek, sliced
½ carrot, sliced
1 medium-sized onion, chopped
1 cup drained canned tomatoes
2 teaspoons salt
1 pound lean beef, cubed
1 pound cabbage, cored and shredded
1 tablespoon lemon juice
½ teaspoon sugar

Heat broth to boiling; add leek, carrot, onion, tomatoes, salt, and meat. Cover and simmer over low heat (about 200° F.) 2 to 2½ hours, or until meat is tender. Remove meat, strain broth if desired. Add cabbage; cook over moderate heat (about 250° F.) until tender, about 10 minutes. Do not overcook. Add lemon juice and sugar. Return meat to pot and heat to serving temperature. For diet serving allow 3 ounces meat and ¼ of the vegetables (287 calories). Serves 4.

German Diet
Menu 1 / 1,196 Calories

BREAKFAST

Citrus cup (½ orange and ½ grapefruit)
1 boiled egg
1 slice whole-grain rye bread

LUNCH

Sandwich: 3 ounces Lachschinken (smoked rolled ham)
2 leaves lettuce
2 slices pumpernickel bread
½ grapefruit

DINNER

*Fladen Soup
*Liver Dumplings
½ cup Sauerkraut OR red cabbage
½ cup water-packed apricot halves

SUPPLEMENTS

1 cup skim milk
1 apple
1 tangerine

* Recipe given

Fladen Soup

¼ cup flour
½ cup skim milk
1 egg, slightly beaten
¼ teaspoon salt

1 quart hot canned chicken broth
Chopped chives or parsley

Mix flour and milk together; stir until smooth. Add egg and salt. Lightly oil a 6-inch skillet; heat pan over moderately high heat (about 325° F.). Pour 3 tablespoons batter into pan and tilt pan to cover bottom with batter. Cook until golden brown on one side. With a spatula, carefully turn and brown other side. Repeat procedure with remaining batter. It may be necessary to re-grease skillet after preparing a few pancakes. Stack pancakes and roll them up together; cut crosswise into thin strips. Divide strips into soup bowls and add hot broth. Garnish with chopped chives or parsley. For diet serving allow ¼ of the pancake strips and 1 cup broth (86 calories). Serves 4.

Liver Dumplings

¼ cup dry bread crumbs
¼ cup skim milk
½ pound beef or calf's liver, ground
1 egg
¼ teaspoon ground marjoram

½ teaspoon salt
1 tablespoon vegetable oil
2 tablespoons finely chopped onion
2 tablespoons finely chopped parsley
1 quart boiling salted water

Mix crumbs and milk in bowl. Add ground liver, egg, marjoram, and salt; mix well. Heat oil in skillet over moderate heat (about 250° F.); add onion and cook until tender. Add parsley and cook 1 minute longer. Fold cooked vegetables into liver and blend well. Chill mixture in refrigerator 8 to 12 hours. In a large saucepan bring to a boil 1 quart salted water. With 2 soup-spoons, scoop out some of the liver mixture and gently spoon into boiling water. Reduce heat to moderately low (about 225° F.) and keep water simmering gently. Cook dumplings 5 minutes after they rise to the surface. Remove with a slotted spoon. Keep in warm oven until all dumplings are made. Repeat procedure with remaining mixture, bringing water to a boil each time before adding more liver mixture. For diet serving allow 5 dumplings (217 calories). Serves 3.

BREAKFAST

½ cup orange juice
2 ounces sprats (herring)
1 slice pumpernickel bread

LUNCH

½ cup cottage cheese and chives
1 thin slice ham
Relish plate: 2 radishes and
4 carrot sticks
2 slices whole-grain rye bread
1 tangerine

DINNER

¼ cup fresh pea soup
*Poached Cod with Mustard Sauce
1 boiled potato
½ cup cooked spinach
½ cup fresh fruit cup (grapes,
orange, banana, and apple)

SUPPLEMENTS

2 cups skim milk
1 small banana

* Recipe given

Poached Cod

1 cup water	1 teaspoon salt
1 tablespoon lemon juice	1 pound cod, halibut, or
4 peppercorns	haddock
½ small onion, thinly sliced	Mustard Sauce (recipe be-
1 bay leaf	low)
1 teaspoon vinegar	

Place all ingredients except fish and Mustard Sauce in saucepan; bring to a boil and simmer over low heat (about 200° F.) 5 minutes. Strain stock; add fish and simmer over low heat (about 200° F.) 10 to 15 minutes, or until fish is easily flaked. Remove fish and keep warm in oven. Strain broth and use in Mustard Sauce (recipe below). Serve fish with Mustard Sauce. For diet serving allow 3 ounces fish with ¼ cup sauce (185 calories). Serves 3 to 4.

Mustard Sauce

1 tablespoon vegetable oil	Fish stock
1 tablespoon finely chopped onion	Skim milk
1 tablespoon flour	1 tablespoon prepared mus-
	tard

Heat oil in saucepan over moderate heat (about 250° F.); add onion and cook until tender. Blend in flour and cook 1 minute. Remove from heat. Measure fish stock and add enough skim milk to make 1 cup liquid. Gradually stir stock into flour mixture. Cook over moderately low heat (about 225° F.), stirring constantly, until thickened. Blend in mustard. Makes 1 cup sauce.

German Diet
Menu 3 / 1,195 Calories

BREAKFAST

½ grapefruit
½ cup cooked farina
1 cup skim milk
1 teaspoon sugar, cinnamon

LUNCH

3 ounces Matjes herring
1 medium-sized onion, sliced
½ dill pickle
2 slices pumpernickel bread
1 apple

DINNER

*Einlaufsuppe
*Veal Stew
2 leaves endive
1 tablespoon bottled low-calorie
French dressing
1 unsweetened baked apple

SUPPLEMENTS

1 cup skim milk
1 pear
1 orange

* Recipe given

Einlaufsuppe

1½ quarts canned chicken or beef broth	1 egg
	1 teaspoon flour

Heat broth to boiling over moderately high heat (about 350° F.). Beat egg and flour together, and gradually pour in a thin steady stream into the boiling broth. Cook for 2 minutes. For diet serving allow 1 cup broth (44 calories). Serves 6.

Veal Stew

2 whole cloves	½ teaspoon salt
1 small onion	1 pound lean veal, cut into 1-inch cubes
1½ cups chicken or beef broth	1 tablespoon cornstarch
1 bay leaf	2 tablespoons water
1 small lemon slice	2 tablespoons dry white wine
1 teaspoon vinegar	

Stick cloves into onion and place in saucepan with broth, bay leaf, lemon, vinegar, and salt; heat to boiling. Add veal and simmer over low heat (about 200° F.) 1½ hours or until fork-tender. Remove meat; strain and skim off fat from broth. Measure broth and add water if necessary to make 1 cup of liquid. Mix cornstarch and the 2 tablespoons water together; gradually add to hot broth. Cook over moderate heat (about 250° F.), stirring constantly, until thickened. Stir in wine. Add cooked veal and heat thoroughly over low heat (about 200° F.), but do not boil. For diet serving allow 3 ounces of meat and ¼ cup sauce (183 calories). Serves 3 to 4.

German Diet
Menu 4 / 1,224 Calories

BREAKFAST
½ cup tomato juice
⅔ cup cooked oatmeal
1 cup skim milk

LUNCH
3 ounces smoked eel, Bückling,
OR flounder
2 slices rye bread
1 medium-sized tomato, sliced
1 pear

DINNER
1 cup beef broth
3 ounces boiled beef with
horse-radish sauce
½ cup cooked Savoy cabbage
½ cup unsweetened applesauce

SUPPLEMENTS
1 cup skim milk
1 tangerine
½ cup grapes

Jewish Diet
Menu 1 / 1,201 Calories

BREAKFAST
1 orange
1 poached egg
1 slice enriched white bread,
toasted

LUNCH
* Herring Salad
*Mock Sour Cream
2 slices pumpernickel bread
Relish plate: 1 slice tomato,
2 slices cucumber, 1 stalk celery,
and 1 radish
½ cup unsweetened applesauce

* Recipe given

[42]

DINNER

Sweet-and-Sour Stuffed Cabbage
½ cup cooked rice
Relish plate: 2 slices green pepper,
small bunch water cress, ¼ cup
pickled beets
½ cup unsweetened pineapple
tidbits

SUPPLEMENTS

2 cups skim milk
1 tangerine
½ cup grapes

Herring Salad

1 cup (8 ounces) herring tidbits or 1 cup fillet of herring	White of 1 hard-cooked egg
1 medium-sized apple, peeled and cored	¼ cup diced dill pickle
1 medium-sized potato, peeled	Few capers
	1½ teaspoons sugar
	Freshly ground pepper

Chop herring, apple, potato, and egg white. Place all ingredients in a bowl and fold together. Chill and serve with Mock Sour Cream (*recipe below*). For diet serving allow 2 ounces herring (87 calories). Serves 3 to 4.

Mock Sour Cream

2 tablespoons lemon juice	1 cup cottage cheese
3 to 5 tablespoons skim milk	Pinch of salt

Place lemon juice and 3 tablespoons skim milk in an electric blender. Gradually add cottage cheese and salt, blending at low speed. Blend a few minutes at high speed until smooth. Thin mixture if necessary with the remaining skim milk. If mixture is too thick on standing, thin with additional milk before serving. For diet serving allow 2 ounces (57 calories). Makes 1 cup mixture.

Sweet-and-Sour Stuffed Cabbage

1 small head cabbage	1 small onion, grated
1 pound ground beef, ground twice	¼ cup soft bread crumbs
	¼ cup water

[43]

½ teaspoon salt	1 cup canned tomatoes
1 small onion, sliced	1 tablespoon lemon juice
1 medium-sized carrot, sliced	2 tablespoons brown sugar
1 cup canned beef consommé	1 teaspoon salt

Cut out and discard core of cabbage. Place cabbage in a large saucepan and cover with boiling water; simmer over low heat (about 200° F.) 5 minutes. Remove from water and carefully remove 8 outer leaves. Cut about 4 slices from the remaining cabbage to use in recipe. Leftover cabbage may be used in another meal. Combine meat, the grated onion, bread crumbs, water, and the ½ teaspoon salt. Fill each cabbage leaf with ¼ cup of the meat filling. Roll up tight and fasten with a toothpick. Place cabbage rolls in a deep saucepan, folded side down; add sliced cabbage, the sliced onion, and carrot. Add consommé. Cook over low heat (about 200° F.) for 1 hour, stirring occasionally. Add tomatoes, lemon juice, brown sugar, and the 1 teaspoon salt. Cook 1 hour longer. Remove cabbage rolls to warm platter; if desired, strain vegetables through a strainer or a food mill. Heat and serve mixture over cabbage. For diet serving allow 2 cabbage rolls and ¼ cup sauce (283 calories). Serves 3 to 4.

Jewish Diet
Menu 2 / 1,176 Calories

BREAKFAST
½ cup apple juice
2 ounces cottage cheese
½ ounce smoked salmon
½ bagel

LUNCH
3 ounces gefilte fish
Horse-radish sauce
1 small boiled potato
½ cup cooked spinach
½ cup fresh fruit cup
(pineapple, banana, orange)

DINNER
1 cup clear bouillon
3 ounces roast veal
* Kasha Varnishkis
½ cup cooked green beans
¼ cup pickled beets and 2 leaves
endive
½ grapefruit

SUPPLEMENTS
1 cup skim milk
1 small banana
½ cup grapes

* Recipe given

Kasha Varnishkis

1 tablespoon vegetable oil	1 medium-sized onion,
½ cup buckwheat groats	minced
½ teaspoon salt	½ pound mushrooms, sliced
1¼ cups water (*about*)	½ teaspoon salt
3 ounces noodle bows	Few grains pepper
1 tablespoon vegetable oil	

Heat the 1 tablespoon oil in a large skillet over moderate heat (about 250° F.); add groats and cook until brown, stirring occasionally. Sprinkle with the ½ teaspoon salt. Add the 1¼ cups water, or as much as groats will absorb. Cover and remove from heat. Heat oven to 350° F. Cook noodles in boiling salted water over moderate heat (about 250° F.) 10 to 12 minutes, or until just tender. Heat the 1 tablespoon oil in a second skillet over moderate heat (about 250° F.); add onions and cook until tender. Add mushrooms and cook 5 minutes. Fold groats, noodles, vegetable mixture, the ½ teaspoon salt, and pepper together; pour into a 1-quart casserole. Bake 20 to 25 minutes. Serve hot. For diet serving allow ½ cup (127 calories). Serves 6 to 8.

Jewish Diet
Menu 3 / 1,191 Calories

BREAKFAST

½ cup orange-and-grapefruit juice
½ cup cooked whole wheat cereal
1 cup skim milk

LUNCH

½ cup tomato juice
*Chopped Chicken Liver
sandwich with rye bread
½ cup fruit-flavored gelatin

DINNER

1 cup borsch
1 ounce Mock Sour Cream
(recipe on page 43)
3 ounces baked whitefish
1 medium-sized boiled potato
½ cup cooked green beans
½ cup cooked carrots
1 stalk celery
1 unsweetened baked apple

SUPPLEMENTS

1 cup skim milk
1 small banana
1 orange

* Recipe given

---

[45]

Chopped Chicken Livers

2 tablespoons vegetable oil
2 small onions, sliced
½ pound chicken livers
2 tablespoons water
2 hard-cooked eggs, chopped

½ teaspoon salt
Few grains pepper
2 to 3 tablespoons chicken broth

Heat oil in skillet over moderate heat (about 200° F.); add onion and cook until tender, stirring occasionally. Add chicken livers and cook until lightly browned. Add water, cover and cook slowly over low heat (about 200° F.) 10 minutes. Cool and chop livers finely. Mix chopped livers, chopped egg, salt, and pepper. Stir in enough chicken broth to moisten mixture. For diet serving allow 2 ounces liver mixture (123 calories). Serves 4.

Jewish Diet
Menu 4 / 1,198 Calories

BREAKFAST
½ grapefruit
2 ounces broiled kippers
½ biali

DINNER
* Stewed Chicken with Matzo Balls
Dried-fruit compote (2 prunes and 2 apricots)

LUNCH
Pumpernickel sandwich of 2 ounces farmer cheese and 6 cucumber slices
1 pear

SUPPLEMENTS
2 cups skim milk
1 apple
½ cup grapes

* Recipe given

Stewed Chicken

1 5½-pound fowl, cut up
1 sprig parsley
1 bay leaf
1 small onion, cut in half
2 small carrots, cut into 1-inch slices

1 stalk celery
½ pound green beans, sliced
½ pound peas, shelled
2½ teaspoons salt
Matzo Balls (recipe below)

Clean and wash fowl; place in a large saucepan with boiling water to cover. Add parsley, bay leaf, onion, carrot, and celery. Cook over low heat (about 200° F.) 1 hour. Add beans, peas, and salt; cover and cook 1 to 1½ hours longer, or until chicken is tender. Remove from heat. Drain and let broth cool. Skim off fat. Heat broth to boiling. Drop matzo ball batter into boiling soup and simmer over moderately low heat (about 225° F.) 15 minutes. Remove balls and add chicken and vegetables and heat to serving temperature. Place cooked matzo balls on top and heat just before serving. For diet serving allow 3 ounces chicken, ¼ cup carrots, ¼ cup peas, ½ cup green beans, broth, and 2 matzo balls (312 calories). Serves 4 to 6.

Matzo Balls

1 cup hot chicken broth	1 egg, slightly beaten
1 cup matzo meal	½ teaspoon salt
2 tablespoons vegetable oil	Few grains ground nutmeg

Pour hot broth over meal; mix well. Add oil, egg, and seasonings; mix until blended. Chill. Form rounded tablespoons of batter into balls. Cook as directed above. Makes 12 balls.

American Diet
Menu 1 / 1,189 Calories

BREAKFAST

1 orange, sliced
⅔ cup cooked oatmeal
1 cup skim milk

LUNCH

3 ounces turkey OR chicken
2 slices white bread
2 leaves lettuce
½ tomato
1 tablespoon bottled low-calorie
French dressing

DINNER

1 cup consommé
3 ounces shrimp OR fish
½ cup cooked rice
½ cup cooked broccoli
1 cup mixed green salad
1 tablespoon bottled low-calorie
French dressing
1 pear

SUPPLEMENTS

1 cup skim milk
1 small banana
½ cup grapes

American Diet
Menu 2 / 1,223 Calories

BREAKFAST

½ cup apple juice
1 ounce corn flakes
1 cup skim milk

LUNCH

Ham sandwich on whole wheat
bread with 3 ounces ham
1 cup mixed green salad
1 tablespoon bottled low-calorie
French dressing
1 apple

DINNER

3 ounces roast veal
½ cup cooked noodles
½ cup cooked diced carrots
1 cup sliced Chinese cabbage
1 tablespoon bottled low-calorie
French dressing
Citrus cup (½ orange and
½ grapefruit)

SUPPLEMENT

1 cup skim milk

American Diet
Menu 3 / 1,182 Calories

BREAKFAST

½ grapefruit
1 poached egg
1 slice white bread

LUNCH

3 ounces canned salmon
2 leaves lettuce
2 slices whole wheat bread
1 pear

DINNER

1 cup bouillon
3 ounces broiled chicken
1 small baked potato
½ cup cooked spinach
Relish plate: 2 radishes, 3 slices
cucumber, and 1 stalk celery
½ cup strawberry-flavored gelatin
with 1 slice water-packed
pineapple

SUPPLEMENTS

2 cups skim milk
1 tangerine
½ cup grapes

BREAKFAST

½ cup orange juice
2 slices broiled Canadian bacon
1 slice whole wheat bread

LUNCH

½ cup cottage cheese
4 medium-sized unsweetened
prunes
Lettuce and water cress
1 tablespoon bottled low-calorie
French dressing
1 slice white bread
½ cup diced fresh unsweetened
pineapple

DINNER

3 ounces steak OR roast beef
½ cup cooked peas
1 broiled tomato
3 large romaine leaves
1 tablespoon bottled low-calorie
French dressing
½ cup unsweetened applesauce

SUPPLEMENTS

2 cups skim milk
1 pear

American Menus and Recipes

HERE is a selection of menus catering to widespread American tastes. Like all the meal plans in the Wise Woman's Diet, these menus are nutritionally balanced to include 25 percent of their total daily calories in proteins, 45 percent in carbohydrates, and 30 percent in fats. You do not have to worry about vitamins—they are all here, as well as all the other nutritional elements necessary to good health.

By following these menus, the dieter is able to eat regular family meals, scaled down to prescribed portions. On this sensible allowance of 1,200 calories a day, most women can lose two or three pounds a week without suffering the monotony, fatigue, or depression that can accompany poorly balanced crash or fad diets.

Perhaps the best thing about the Wise Woman's Diet is that it helps you toward your true long-range goal of learning good eating habits. Once you do, you can stay at your ideal weight forever, instead of always fluctuating back and forth. As a bonus, you can help your husband and children establish the same good habits that may prevent future weight problems for them.

Menu 1 / 1,194 Calories

BREAKFAST

½ grapefruit
1 poached egg
1 slice whole wheat bread

LUNCH

3 ounces canned tuna
2 lettuce leaves
2 slices tomato
1 stalk celery
1 slice enriched white bread
½ cup lime-flavored gelatin

DINNER

1 cup cream of mushroom soup
*Veal with Herb Sauce
1 broiled tomato
½ cup cooked broccoli
1 apple

SUPPLEMENTS

2 cups skim milk
1 orange

* Recipe given

Veal with Herb Sauce

1 tablespoon vegetable oil	⅔ cup water
1 pound veal for scallopini	1½ tablespoons lemon juice
2 medium-sized onions, thinly sliced	¾ teaspoon salt
1 clove garlic, mashed (optional)	¼ teaspoon dried oregano leaves

Heat oil in a skillet over moderately high heat (about 300° F.); add veal slices and brown quickly on both sides. Remove veal from skillet. Reduce heat to moderate (about 250° F.) and cook onions and garlic until tender but not brown, stirring frequently. Return veal to skillet with the water, lemon juice, salt, and oregano; cover and cook over moderately low heat (about 225° F.) for 20 minutes, turning frequently, until veal is tender. For diet serving allow 3 ounces veal and ¼ of the sauce (239 calories). Serves 4.

[51]

BREAKFAST

1 orange, sliced
1 ounce corn flakes
1 cup skim milk

LUNCH

*Pepper Pot Soup
Relish plate: 2 radishes, 1 celery
stalk, and 4 carrot sticks
2 slices enriched white bread
½ cup water-packed apricot halves

DINNER

*Swiss Steak
½ cup cooked noodles
½ cup cooked sliced carrots
1 cup mixed green salad
1 tablespoon * Low-Calorie French
Dressing
½ cup unsweetened applesauce

SUPPLEMENTS

1 cup skim milk
1 apple
2 dried prunes

* Recipe given

Pepper Pot Soup

½ pound honeycomb tripe, cut into ½-inch cubes	⅛ teaspoon pepper
1 pound veal neck, sliced	1 cup canned tomatoes
1 quart water	¼ cup chopped onion
Pinch of dried thyme leaves	½ cup diced carrot
¼ teaspoon dried oregano leaves	½ cup diced celery
¼ teaspoon dried basil leaves	½ cup chopped green pepper
1¾ teaspoon salt	½ cup diced potato
	1½ tablespoons chopped parsley

Place tripe, veal, water, thyme, oregano, basil, salt, and pepper in a Dutch oven. Cover and bring to a boil over moderately high heat (about 300° F.); reduce heat to moderately low (about 225° F.) and cook 2½ to 3 hours, or until tripe is fork-tender. Remove from heat; cool; then chill in refrigerator several hours or overnight to allow fat to harden. Discard fat. Add tomatoes, onion, carrot, celery, green pepper, and potato; place over moderately high heat (about 300° F.) until boiling. Reduce heat to moderately low (about 225° F.) and cook ½ hour. Remove veal bones from soup and cut meat from

[52]

bones into small pieces. Add meat and parsley to soup. For diet serving allow 1 cup soup (184 calories). Makes about 1½ quarts, or 4 to 6 servings.

Swiss Steak

1½ pounds chuck steak, cut ½ inch thick	½ cup chopped celery
Unseasoned instant meat tenderizer	½ teaspoon ground marjoram
Salt and pepper	¼ teaspoon garlic powder
1 16-ounce can tomatoes	¾ teaspoon salt
1 medium-sized onion, thinly sliced	⅛ teaspoon pepper

Cut off all visible fat from steak. Cook pieces of fat in a heavy skillet over moderately low heat (about 225° F.) until fat is released. Discard unmelted fat. Sprinkle meat with meat tenderizer, following directions on jar; then sprinkle with salt and pepper. Brown lightly in the fat in skillet over moderately high heat (about 300° F.). Pour off excess fat. Add remaining ingredients. Cover and cook over low heat (about 200° F.) 2½ hours, or until fork-tender. Add water during cooking if too much liquid evaporates. For diet serving allow 3 ounces meat and ¼ of the sauce (204 calories). Serves 4.

Low-Calorie French Dressing

2 tablespoons flour	½ teaspoon paprika
1 cup water	½ teaspoon Worcestershire sauce
¼ cup catsup	1 teaspoon sugar
1 teaspoon prepared horse-radish	½ cup vinegar
1 teaspoon dry mustard	1 clove garlic (optional)

Put flour in a small saucepan. Slowly stir in water. Cook over moderately low heat (about 225° F.), stirring constantly, until thickened and smooth, about 5 minutes. Cool. Add remaining ingredients except garlic. Beat with a rotary beater until well blended. Pour into a storage container; add garlic, if desired. Cover and store in refrigerator. Shake well before using. For diet serving allow 1 tablespoon dressing (5 calories). Makes 1¾ cups.

Variation: For an herb dressing, omit horse-radish, mustard, and garlic, and substitute ¼ teaspoon dried thyme leaves, ¼ teaspoon powdered marjoram, and a pinch of dried rosemary leaves.

BREAKFAST

½ grapefruit
1 poached egg
1 slice enriched white bread

LUNCH

Ham sandwich on whole wheat
bread with 3 ounces ham
1 cup mixed green salad
*1 tablespoon * Low-Calorie Salad*
Dressing
½ cup diced fresh pineapple,
unsweetened

DINNER

* Onion Soup
*Crisp Baked Chicken
½ cup cooked broccoli
½ cup mashed cooked squash
⅛ head lettuce
*1 tablespoon * Low-Calorie Salad*
Dressing
⅔ cup water-packed sliced peaches

SUPPLEMENT

2 cups skim milk

* *Recipe given*

Low-Calorie Salad Dressing

⅔ cup nonfat dry milk solids

¾ teaspoon unflavored gelatine

1 teaspoon salt

⅛ teaspoon dry mustard

Dash of cayenne pepper

1 cup boiling water

2 egg yolks, slightly beaten

2 tablespoons lemon juice

Combine dry milk solids, gelatin, salt, dry mustard, and cayenne pepper in the top of a double boiler. Gradually stir in the boiling water. Slowly add about half the hot mixture to the beaten yolks. Combine thoroughly and return to top of double boiler. Place over boiling water. Cook, stirring constantly, until thickened and smooth. Remove from heat and stir in lemon juice. Cool. Dressing may be stored in refrigerator for several days. Beat with a rotary beater before using. For diet serving allow 1 tablespoon dressing (15 calories). Makes 1¼ cups.

Onion Soup

1 tablespoon butter or margarine

6 large onions, sliced

2 beef bouillon cubes

4 cups hot water

¼ cup grated Parmesan cheese

[54]

Melt butter in a heavy saucepan over moderate heat (about 250° F.). Add onions and cook until soft and golden brown. Dissolve bouillon cubes in the hot water. Add to onions. Cook over moderately low heat (about 225° F.) for 10 minutes. Pour into serving dishes; sprinkle with 1 tablespoon cheese. For diet serving allow 1 cup soup (115 calories). Serves 4.

Crisp Baked Chicken

1	2½-to-3-pound broiler-fryer chicken, cut in half	¼	teaspoon salt Dash of pepper
6	tablespoons commercial sour cream	4	teaspoons packaged cereal crumbs
2	tablespoons lemon juice		Dash of paprika
½	teaspoon crushed dried rosemary leaves	1	tablespoon parsley

Heat oven to 375° F. Wash and dry chicken. Blend sour cream, lemon juice, rosemary, salt, and pepper. Spread half the sour cream mixture over chicken and arrange in a shallow baking dish; bake uncovered about 50 minutes, or until fork-tender. Brush with remaining sour cream mixture. Sprinkle with crumbs and paprika; continue to bake 10 minutes longer. Garnish with parsley. For diet serving allow 3 ounces chicken with topping (154 calories). Serves 4.

Menu 4 / 1,197 Calories

BREAKFAST
½ cup orange juice
1 ounce bran flakes
1 cup skim milk

LUNCH
* Swiss Luncheon Custards
Relish plate: 1 celery stalk, 3 slices cucumber, ½ carrot (sliced into sticks)
1 slice enriched white bread
1 pear

DINNER
* Savory Chicken Livers
½ cup cooked diced carrots
½ cup cooked spinach
3 large romaine leaves
1 tablespoon * Low-Calorie French Dressing (see page 53)
½ cup water-packed pineapple chunks

SUPPLEMENTS
1 cup skim milk
1 orange

* Recipe given

---

[55]

Swiss Luncheon Custards

4 egg yolks
1⅓ cups skim milk
1½ cups coarsely shredded Swiss cheese
½ teaspoon prepared mustard
⅛ teaspoon Worcestershire sauce
¼ teaspoon salt
4 egg whites, stiffly beaten

Heat oven to 350° F. Beat egg yolks well with a rotary beater; add skim milk, cheese, mustard, Worcestershire sauce, and salt. Fold in stiffly beaten egg whites. Pour into 4 greased, deep, 10-ounce pie dishes (about 1¾ inches deep). Place in a large baking pan; add 1-inch warm water to pan. Bake 40 minutes, or until custard is just set in the center. For diet serving allow 1 custard (268 calories). Serves 4.

Savory Chicken Livers

2 tablespoons butter or margarine
1 pound chicken livers
2 chicken bouillon cubes
1½ cups boiling water
½ pound mushrooms, sliced
½ teaspoon salt
Pinch of dried rosemary leaves
A few grains pepper
2 tablespoons cornstarch
2 tablespoons water

Heat butter in a skillet over moderate heat (about 250° F.). Add chicken livers and cook until lightly browned, turning frequently. Dissolve bouillon cubes in the boiling water. Add bouillon, mushrooms, salt, rosemary, and pepper to livers. Cover and cook over moderately low heat (about 225° F.) for 10 minutes, or until chicken livers are cooked through. Mix cornstarch and the 2 tablespoons water together and stir into liquid in pan; cook 5 minutes, stirring constantly. For diet serving allow 3 ounces chicken livers and ¼ of the sauce (266 calories). Serves 4.

Menu 5 / 1,195 Calories

BREAKFAST	LUNCH
1 orange, sliced	*Puffed Spanish Omelet
⅔ cup cooked oatmeal	1 slice whole wheat bread
1 cup skim milk	1 pear

* Recipe given

[56]

DINNER	SUPPLEMENTS
1 cup consommé	1 cup skim milk
*Lamb Curry	1 tangerine
½ cup cooked rice	4 dried prunes
½ cup cooked green beans	
1 cup sliced Chinese cabbage	
1 tablespoon * Low-Calorie French	
Dressing (see page 53)	
½ grapefruit	

Puffed Spanish Omelet

- ½ cup chopped onion
- ½ cup chopped green pepper
- ½ cup chopped celery
- ¾ cup water
- 4 eggs, separated
- ½ cup drained canned tomatoes, chopped
- ½ cup nonfat dry milk solids
- ½ teaspoon dried basil leaves
- 1 teaspoon salt
- Dash of pepper
- 1 tablespoon butter or margarine

Heat oven to 325° F. Combine onion, green pepper, celery, and water in a saucepan. Simmer 15 to 20 minutes over moderately low heat (about 225° F.), or until tender. Drain. Beat egg whites in a large bowl until stiff but not dry. In another large bowl beat egg yolks until thick and lemon-colored. Add tomatoes, dry milk solids, basil, salt, and pepper to egg yolks; beat until blended. Fold in cooked vegetables and beaten egg whites. In a heavy 8-inch skillet with an ovenproof handle, melt butter over moderately high heat (about 275° F.) until butter starts to foam. Add egg mixture and cook 10 minutes, or until omelet puffs up and is lightly browned on the bottom. Place omelet in oven and bake 15 to 17 minutes, until top is dry and lightly browned. Cut into wedges to serve. For diet serving allow ¼ of the omelet (163 calories). Serves 3 to 4.

Lamb Curry

- 1¼ pounds lean, boneless lamb, cubed
- ½ cup chopped onion
- 1 clove garlic, mashed
- 2 cups water
- 1 16-ounce can unsweetened applesauce
- 2 beef bouillon cubes

½ teaspoon salt	1 tablespoon cornstarch
1¼ teaspoons curry powder	1 tablespoon water

Place lamb, onion, garlic, the 2 cups water, applesauce, bouillon cubes, salt, and curry powder in a saucepan over moderately high heat (about 300° F.); cover and heat until mixture comes to a boil. Reduce heat to moderately low (about 225° F.) and cook 1½ hours, or until meat is fork-tender; add additional water if necessary. Mix the cornstarch and the 1 tablespoon water together and stir into lamb mixture; continue cooking until sauce is thickened, stirring constantly. For diet serving allow 3 ounces lamb and ¼ of the sauce (228 calories). Serves 4.

Menu 6 / 1,186 Calories

BREAKFAST
½ cup grapefruit juice
⅔ cup cooked oatmeal
1 cup skim milk

LUNCH
½ cup cottage cheese
½ tomato, sliced
1 lettuce leaf
½ carrot, cut into sticks
2 slices pumpernickel bread
½ cup raspberry-flavored gelatin

DINNER
1 cup chicken OR beef broth
*Fillet of Sole Veronique
½ cup sliced cooked beets
6 frozen asparagus spears, cooked
1 cup mixed green salad
1 tablespoon * Low-Calorie Salad
Dressing (see page 54)
1 unsweetened baked apple

SUPPLEMENTS
1 cup skim milk
1 small banana

* Recipe given

Fillet of Sole Veronique

1 pound fillet of sole, fresh or frozen	1 tablespoon butter or margarine
Salt and pepper	2 tablespoons flour
¼ cup dry white wine	¾ cup skim milk
¼ cup canned chicken broth	½ cup seedless white grapes
1½ teaspoons lemon juice	

Heat oven to 350° F. Place fish in a shallow, lightly oiled baking dish. Sprinkle with salt and pepper. Mix wine, chicken broth, and lemon juice together and pour over fish. Cover and bake 15 minutes. While fish is baking, melt butter in a small saucepan over moderately low heat (about 225° F.). Remove from heat and blend in flour. Gradually add skim milk and cook over moderately low heat, stirring constantly, until thickened. Remove fish from oven and drain juices from baking dish into cream sauce, stirring until blended. Pour sauce over fish and sprinkle with grapes. Place in preheated broiler about 4 inches from heat for about 5 minutes, or until sauce starts to brown. For diet serving allow 3 ounces fish and ¼ of the sauce (291 calories). Serves 4.

Menu 7 / 1,199 Calories

BREAKFAST
½ cup apple juice
1 ounce puffed wheat
1 cup skim milk

LUNCH
3 ounces hamburger on a bun
1 cup mixed green salad
*1 tablespoon * Low-Calorie Salad Dressing (see page 54)*
1 tangerine

DINNER
½ cup tomato soup
*Chicken Florentine
½ cup cooked sliced carrots
1 slice French bread
* Peaches in Sherry

SUPPLEMENTS
1 cup skim milk
1 orange

* *Recipe given*

Chicken Florentine

1 2½-to-3-pound broiler-fryer chicken, quartered
Salt and pepper
2 tablespoons bottled low-calorie Italian-style French dressing
1 4-ounce can mushroom slices
¼ cup flour
1½ cups skim milk
¼ teaspoon salt
A few grains pepper
¾ teaspoon seasoned salt
1 chicken bouillon cube
2 10-ounce packages frozen chopped spinach, cooked
2 tablespoons grated Parmesan cheese

[59]

Sprinkle chicken with salt and pepper. Place skin side down on rack in broiler pan; brush lightly with some of the French dressing. Place in broiler about 5 to 6 inches from heat. Broil 20 to 25 minutes; turn and brush with remaining dressing and meat juices from pan. Broil an additional 20 to 25 minutes, or until fork-tender. While chicken is broiling, prepare sauce. Drain mushrooms and reserve liquid. In a saucepan mix flour and liquid from mushrooms. Gradually add skim milk and beat with a rotary beater to blend. Cook over moderate heat (about 250° F.), stirring constantly, until thickened. Add the ¼ teaspoon salt, pepper, seasoned salt, and bouillon cube. Stir over moderately low heat (about 225° F.) until bouillon cube is dissolved. Add mushrooms. Spoon well-drained cooked spinach into a heatproof baking dish. Arrange chicken over spinach. Top with mushroom sauce and Parmesan cheese. Broil 3 to 4 inches from heat for 3 to 5 minutes. For diet serving allow 3 ounces chicken, ½ cup spinach, and ¼ of the sauce (219 calories). Serves 4.

Peaches in Sherry

1 16-ounce can water-packed peach halves	¼ teaspoon ground cinnamon
	⅛ teaspoon ground nutmeg
2 tablespoons sherry	¼ cup toasted flaked coconut

Drain peaches, reserving juice. Mix together juice, sherry, cinnamon, and nutmeg. Pour over peaches and chill. Serve garnished with coconut. For diet serving allow ¼ of the peaches (88 calories). Serves 3 to 4.

Menu 8 / 1,179 Calories

BREAKFAST

½ cup unsweetened grapefruit juice
½ cup cooked farina
1 cup skim milk

LUNCH

½ cup cottage cheese
6 cucumber slices
2 slices pumpernickel bread
1 orange

DINNER

1 cup consommé
1 lean lamb chop (2 x 1½ x ¾ inches)
1 small baked potato
½ cup cooked spinach
Relish plate: 2 radishes, 4 celery
sticks, 5 carrot sticks
Dried fruit compote: 2 cooked
prunes, 2 cooked apricots

SUPPLEMENTS

2 cups skim milk
1 apple
1 small banana

Menu 9 / 1,199 Calories

BREAKFAST

½ grapefruit
1 poached egg
1 slice white bread

LUNCH

3 ounces canned tuna
2 lettuce leaves
2 slices whole wheat bread
½ cup fresh fruit cup (pineapple,
banana, and orange)

DINNER

3 ounces broiled chicken
½ cup mashed, cooked squash
½ cup cooked peas
⅛ head lettuce
1 tablespoon bottled low-calorie
French dressing
½ cup water-packed apricot halves

SUPPLEMENTS

2 cups skim milk
1 small banana
1 pear

Menu 10 / 1,193 Calories

BREAKFAST

½ cup orange juice
1 soft-cooked egg
1 slice white bread

LUNCH

½ cup cottage cheese
¼ small honeydew melon
1 slice water-packed pineapple
1 slice whole wheat bread
½ cup raspberry-flavored gelatin

DINNER

½ grapefruit
3 ounces broiled beef liver
½ cup cooked sliced green beans
½ cup cooked diced carrots
1 cup mixed green salad
1 tablespoon bottled low-calorie
French dressing
½ cup unsweetened applesauce

SUPPLEMENTS

2 cups skim milk
1 pear
½ cup grapes

Menu 11 / 1,192 Calories

BREAKFAST

½ small honeydew melon
1 ounce bran flakes
1 cup skim milk

LUNCH

1 frankfurter
¼ cup cottage cheese
½ tomato
1 cup mixed green salad
1 tablespoon bottled low-calorie
French dressing
1 orange

DINNER

½ cup unsweetened frozen
pineapple juice
3 ounces broiled ham steak
1 broiled tomato
½ cup cooked broccoli
1 cup mixed green salad
1 tablespoon bottled low-calorie
French dressing
1 unsweetened baked apple

SUPPLEMENTS

1 cup skim milk
1 pear
½ cup grapes

Menu 12 / 1,155 Calories

BREAKFAST

½ grapefruit
⅔ cup cooked oatmeal
1 cup skim milk

LUNCH

3 ounces canned salmon
2 lettuce leaves
½ small tomato
2 slices whole wheat bread
½ cup water-packed pineapple
chunks

DINNER

½ cup tomato juice
3 ounces boiled beef with
horseradish
½ cup cooked cabbage
½ cup cooked diced carrots
1 pear

SUPPLEMENTS

1 cup skim milk
1 small banana
1 orange

Menu 13 / 1,193 Calories

BREAKFAST
1 orange, sliced
½ cup cottage cheese
1 slice whole wheat bread

LUNCH
3 ounces chicken
2 slices white bread
2 lettuce leaves
½ tomato
1 tablespoon bottled low-calorie
French dressing

DINNER
½ cup tomato soup
3 ounces roast veal
½ cup cooked spinach
1 ounce French bread
Relish plate: 1 slice tomato,
3 slices cucumber, 1 stalk celery
⅔ cup water-packed peaches with
2 ounces red wine

SUPPLEMENT
2 cups skim milk

Menu 14 / 1,206 Calories

BREAKFAST
Citrus cup (½ small orange and
½ small grapefruit, sectioned)
1 soft-cooked egg
1 slice whole-grain rye bread

LUNCH
3 ounces hamburger on a bun
1 cup mixed green salad
1 tablespoon bottled low-calorie
French dressing
1 pear

DINNER
3 ounces poached fillet of sole
½ cup cooked rice
½ cup peas cooked with ½ cup
shredded Boston lettuce
3 large romaine lettuce leaves
1 tablespoon bottled low-calorie
French dressing
½ small honeydew melon

SUPPLEMENTS
1 cup skim milk
1 apple
½ cup grapes

Fourteen-Day Wise Woman's Diet

HERE are two weeks of menus that include dishes that are delectable enough to serve to company. Instead of martyring yourself over a miniature hamburger while your family and friends dine on lasagna, you eat what everyone else does—like a delicious recipe for Beef Stroganoff that uses a diet version of sour cream that would fool a tsar, or a marvelous Oriental specialty like Chinese Beef. You eat only as much as is recommended in each menu, staying close to the 1,200-calories-per-day limit, and let the non-dieters eat as much as they wish.

Another feature in this series of menus is take-with lunches for the working woman who dreads the daily battle of the breadbasket and other restaurant enticements. For five days of each week's menus, there are lunches that can be eaten at home or packed to take along to work.

This fourteen-day edition of the Wise Woman's Diet is planned to start on Sunday. If you wish to start on Monday, begin with that day and come back to Sunday at the end of the two weeks.

Sunday / Menu 1

With Lunch at Home / 1,197 Calories

BREAKFAST

½ cup orange juice
1 poached egg
1 slice enriched white bread

LUNCH

*Steak Tartare
Relish plate: ½ carrot and ½ stalk
celery, cut into sticks
⅔ cup water-packed pears

DINNER

*Chicken Baked in Wine
½ cup cooked rice
½ cup cooked diced beets
3 large romaine leaves
1 tablespoon *Catsup Yoghurt
Dressing
*Coffee Fluff

SUPPLEMENTS

2 cups skim milk
1 small banana
1 tangerine

* Recipe given

Steak Tartare

1 egg yolk	1 tablespoon drained capers
1 pound lean ground beef round	½ teaspoon salt
	⅛ teaspoon pepper
2 teaspoons grated onion	4 slices rye bread
1 teaspoon prepared horse-radish	¼ cup chopped parsley

Beat egg yolk slightly and mix with beef, onion, horseradish, capers, salt, and pepper. Spread a quarter of the meat mixture over each slice of bread. Sprinkle chopped parsley around edge of bread. If desired, garnish with a few capers in the center. For diet serving allow 1 slice of bread spread with the meat mixture. About 280 calories. Serves 4.

Chicken Baked in Wine

1 3½-pound broiler-fryer chicken, quartered Seasoned salt	¼ cup dry white wine
	1 cup canned chicken broth

[65]

1 teaspoon instant minced onion	1 4-ounce can sliced mushrooms, drained
1/2 teaspoon curry powder	4 water chestnuts, thinly sliced
1/4 cup water	
2 tablespoons flour	

Heat oven to 350° F. Wash and dry chicken and remove any visible fat. Sprinkle chicken on both sides with seasoned salt; place in a shallow 1½-quart baking dish, skin side down. Mix together wine, chicken broth, onion, and curry powder; pour over chicken. Cover and bake 30 minutes. Uncover, turn chicken pieces, and continue to bake 30 minutes more, or until fork-tender. Remove chicken to a warm platter. Skim off any fat from meat juices. Place water and flour in a covered jar and shake until blended. Stir flour mixture into meat juices, add mushrooms and water chestnuts. Cook over moderately low heat (about 225° F.), stirring constantly, until gravy is thickened. Serve over chicken. For diet serving allow 3 ounces boned chicken and ¼ of the sauce (about 6 tablespoons). About 180 calories. Serves 4.

Catsup Yoghurt Dressing

1 cup plain yoghurt	1/4 teaspoon salt
1/4 cup catsup	Few grains pepper
1/2 teaspoon prepared horse-radish	1/4 teaspoon dried chives
1/4 teaspoon Worcestershire sauce	1/8 teaspoon dried oregano leaves
	1/8 teaspoon dried rosemary leaves, crushed

Combine all ingredients and blend well. Chill before serving. Can be stored in refrigerator about 1 week. About 11 calories per tablespoon. Makes 1¼ cups.

Coffee Fluff

1 envelope unflavored gelatine	Dash ground nutmeg
1 tablespoon instant coffee powder	1 cup skim milk
1/4 cup sugar	1 teaspoon vanilla extract
	2 egg whites

Mix together in a small saucepan gelatine, coffee powder, sugar, and nutmeg. Stir in milk. Place over low heat (about 200° F.) and heat until gelatine and sugar are dissolved, stirring constantly. Remove from heat. Stir in vanilla and chill until the consistency of unbeaten egg white, stirring occasionally. Meanwhile beat egg whites until stiff but not dry. Fold into gelatine mixture. Turn into a 3-cup mold or individual molds, as desired. Chill until firm. For diet serving allow ½ cup. About 55 calories. Serves 4 to 6.

Monday / Menu 2

With Lunch at Home / 1,192 Calories
With Lunch to Carry / 1,206 Calories

BREAKFAST

½ grapefruit
⅔ cup cooked oatmeal
1 cup skim milk

LUNCH / AT HOME

*Stuffed Tomato Salad
2 lettuce leaves
2 slices process American cheese
1 slice Italian bread
½ cup water-packed canned apricot halves

LUNCH / TO CARRY

Roast beef sandwich (2 slices rye bread with 3 ounces sliced beef)
1 celery stalk
1 tangerine

DINNER

1 cup clear beef broth
*Broiled Fillet of Sole with Cheese Sauce
½ cup cooked sliced carrots
10 small inner chicory leaves
1 tablespoon * Catsup Yoghurt Dressing (see page 66)
1 unsweetened baked apple

SUPPLEMENTS

1 cup skim milk
1 orange
1 pear

* Recipe given

Stuffed Tomato Salad

2 medium-sized tomatoes	¼ cup coarsely chopped celery
Salt and pepper	3 tablespoons commercial sour cream
2 tablespoons finely chopped onion	¼ teaspoon dried basil leaves
¼ cup coarsely chopped cucumber	⅛ teaspoon salt
	2 lettuce leaves

Cut a thin slice from stem end of each tomato and scoop out most of tomato pulp, leaving shells. Drain and sprinkle insides with salt and pepper. Coarsely chop the tomato pulp and mix with onion, cucumber, celery, sour cream, basil, and the ⅛ teaspoon salt. Spoon into tomato shells and chill before serving on lettuce. For diet serving allow 1 tomato and 1 lettuce leaf. About 93 calories. Serves 2.

Broiled Fillet of Sole with Cheese Sauce

2 10-ounce packages frozen broccoli spears	1⅓ cups coarsely shredded Cheddar cheese
1½ pounds fillet of sole or flounder	⅓ cup skim milk
1 tablespoon butter or margarine	½ teaspoon prepared mustard
1 tablespoon lemon juice Salt and pepper	½ teaspoon Worcestershire sauce

Cook broccoli according to package directions until almost tender. Preheat broiler. Place fish fillets in a shallow baking dish or oven-proof platter. Dot with butter and sprinkle with lemon juice, salt, and pepper. Place in broiler about 3 to 4 inches from heat and broil 8 to 10 minutes, or until fish is easily flaked with a fork. While fish is cooking, place cheese and milk in the top of a double boiler over simmering water and cook, stirring constantly, until cheese is melted and sauce is blended. Stir in mustard and Worcestershire. Arrange broccoli around cooked fillets and pour cheese sauce over both fish and broccoli. Place under broiler for 1 to 2 minutes, or until sauce starts to brown. For diet serving allow 3 ounces fish with ¼ of sauce and ½ cup broccoli. About 227 calories. Serves 4.

Tuesday / Menu 3

With Lunch at Home / 1,192 Calories
With Lunch to Carry / 1,197 Calories

BREAKFAST

½ cup orange-and-grapefruit juice
½ cup cooked whole wheat cereal
1 cup skim milk

LUNCH / AT HOME

Chicken sandwich (2 slices enriched white bread, 3 ounces sliced chicken, 2 lettuce leaves, and ½ tomato, sliced)
⅔ cup water-packed sliced peaches

LUNCH / TO CARRY

*Chicken sandwich (2 slices
enriched white bread, 3 ounces
sliced chicken, and 2 lettuce leaves)
5 carrot sticks
1 tangerine*

DINNER

**Pink Lady Consommé
*Hamburger Balls with
Onion Sauce
*Dilled Cabbage (2 wedges)
½ cup cooked sliced carrots
⅛ head lettuce
1 tablespoon *Catsup Yoghurt
Dressing (see page 66)
1 pear*

SUPPLEMENTS

*1 cup skim milk
½ cup grapes*

* *Recipe given*

Pink Lady Consommé

1 12½-ounce can jellied consommé madrilene
1 soup can buttermilk

1 tablespoon lemon juice
Cut fresh dill

Mix consommé and buttermilk. Stir in lemon juice. Chill several hours. For diet serving allow ¼ of the consommé with a sprinkling of dill. About 46 calories. For nondieters, top each serving of consommé with 1 tablespoon commercial sour cream, if desired. Serves 4.

Hamburger Balls with Onion Sauce

1 tablespoon instant minced
   onion
1 tablespoon water
1 pound lean ground beef
1 tablespoon chopped par-
   sley
1 egg
½ teaspoon salt
1 tablespoon vegetable oil

3 tablespoons butter or
   margarine
5 medium-sized onions,
   thinly sliced
¼ pound mushrooms, sliced
½ teaspoon salt
1 cup canned beef con-
   sommé

Sprinkle onion over water and let stand 5 minutes to hydrate. Mix together meat, onion, parsley, egg, and the ½ teaspoon salt. Shape heaping table-

[69]

spoonfuls of meat into balls. There should be about 15 balls. Heat oil in a skillet over moderately high heat (about 275° F.); brown meat balls on all sides. Remove balls from skillet. Melt butter in skillet over moderately low heat (about 225° F.); add onions and cook until transparent and golden brown. Add mushrooms, the ½ teaspoon salt, and beef consommé; mix together. Add browned meat balls; cover and heat over moderately low heat for 20 minutes. For diet serving allow 3 meat balls and ¼ of the sauce. About 344 calories. Serves 4.

Dilled Cabbage

1 small cabbage (about 1½ pounds), cut into 8 wedges	⅛ teaspoon dillseed
½ teaspoon salt	Dash of Tabasco
	Water

Arrange cabbage wedges in a wide-bottomed saucepan. Sprinkle with salt, dillseed, and Tabasco. Add water to a depth of 1 inch. Place over moderately high heat (about 275° F.) and bring to a quick boil. Reduce heat to low (about 200° F.); cover and simmer 10 to 15 minutes, or until crisp-tender. Drain. For diet serving allow 2 wedges (weighing a total of about 4½ ounces). About 24 calories. Serves 4.

Wednesday / Menu 4
With Lunch at Home or to Carry / 1,189 Calories

BREAKFAST
½ cup orange-and-grapefruit juice
1 cooked egg
1 slice white bread

LUNCH
*Individual Meat Loaves
1 slice whole wheat bread
4 radishes
1 stalk celery
1 apple

DINNER
*Sweetbreads in Wine
½ cup cooked rice
6 cooked asparagus spears
⅛ head lettuce
1 tablespoon *Catsup Yoghurt Dressing (see page 66)
½ cup orange-flavored-gelatin dessert
⅓ cup water-packed fruit cocktail

SUPPLEMENTS
2 cups skim milk
1 tangerine

* Recipe given

Individual Meat Loaves

1 tablespoon water
1 tablespoon instant minced
   onion
1 pound ground lean beef
   round
1 egg, slightly beaten
¼ cup seasoned bread
   crumbs

1 teaspoon prepared horse-
   radish
½ teaspoon salt
   Few grains pepper
¼ cup bottled barbecue
   sauce

Heat oven to 350° F. Mix water and onion together and let stand 1 minute. Mix ground beef, egg, bread crumbs, horse-radish, salt, and pepper together. Shape into 4 individual meat loaves and place in a small baking dish. Brush with barbecue sauce and bake 15 minutes; brush again with sauce. Bake 15 minutes longer and brush once more with sauce. Continue baking 15 minutes more, allowing 45 minutes for complete baking time. (Cool and chill if wrapping for lunch box.) For diet serving allow 1 loaf. About 201 calories. Serves 4.

Sweetbreads in Wine

2 pairs sweetbreads
   Boiling water
1 teaspoon salt
1 cup canned chicken broth
1 medium-sized onion, sliced
1 medium-sized carrot, sliced
3 sprigs parsley

1 bay leaf
   Pinch dried thyme leaves
½ teaspoon salt
½ cup dry white wine
1 tablespoon water
1 tablespoon cornstarch

Drop sweetbreads into boiling water to cover; add the 1 teaspoon salt. Cover and cook over low heat (about 200° F.) for 25 minutes. While sweet-breads are cooking, place chicken broth, onion, carrot, parsley, bay leaf, thyme, and the ½ teaspoon salt in a small saucepan. Cook over low heat (about 200° F.) for 15 minutes, or until vegetables are almost tender. Heat oven to 350° F. Drain sweetbreads; hold them under cold running water and slip off the thin outside membrane with your fingers. With a paring knife cut out any dark veins and thick connective tissue. Place sweetbreads in a shallow 1½-quart baking dish. Stir wine into the vegetable broth mixture and pour over sweetbreads. Cover and bake 20 minutes; uncover and bake 10 minutes longer. Place sweetbreads on a warm platter. Remove parsley and pour vegetable-broth mixture into a small saucepan. Blend the water and cornstarch together and stir into vegetable mixture. Cook over moderately low heat (about 225° F.) until mixture thickens, stirring constantly. Serve over sweetbreads. For diet serving allow 3 ounces sweetbreads and ¼ of the vegetable sauce (about ⅓ cup). About 217 calories. Serves 4.

Thursday / Menu 5
With Lunch at Home or to Carry / 1,193 Calories

BREAKFAST
1 orange, sliced
½ cup cooked farina
1 cup skim milk

LUNCH / AT HOME OR TO CARRY
**Hearty Clam Chowder*
1 small roll
1 ounce Swiss cheese
Relishes: 1 stalk celery, ½ carrot, and 2 radishes
1 apple

DINNER
½ cup tomato juice
**Beef Stroganoff*
½ cup cooked noodles
**Parsley Zucchini*
*1 tablespoon * Buttermilk-Herb Dressing*
½ cup diced unsweetened fresh pineapple

SUPPLEMENTS
1 cup skim milk
1 tangerine

* Recipe given

Hearty Clam Chowder

1 10½-ounce can whole clams	1 medium-sized potato, diced
½ cup coarsely chopped onion	1 cup stewed tomatoes
½ cup coarsely chopped green pepper	1 cup water
½ cup coarsely chopped celery	½ teaspoon dried thyme leaves
½ cup finely diced carrot	1 teaspoon salt
	Few grains pepper

Drain clams and pour juice into a saucepan. Add onion, green pepper, celery, carrot, potato, tomatoes, water, thyme, salt, and pepper to saucepan. Cover and cook over moderately low heat (about 225° F.) 20 to 25 minutes, or until vegetables are tender. Cut clams in half and add to chowder; heat 5 minutes. For diet serving allow 1 cup chowder. About 84 calories. Makes 1 quart, or serves 4.

Beef Stroganoff

1 tablespoon commercial sour cream	1 can condensed onion soup
½ cup buttermilk	¼ cup dry white wine
1½ pounds beef sirloin	¾ cup water
½ tablespoon butter or margarine	¼ teaspoon dried dillweed
½ pound mushrooms, thinly sliced	⅛ teaspoon pepper
	1 tablespoon flour

Blend sour cream and buttermilk and let stand at room temperature while preparing rest of recipe. Slice meat thin and remove as much fat as possible. Heat butter in a medium-sized skillet over moderate heat (about 250° F.). Add mushrooms and cook 5 to 6 minutes, or until mushrooms begin to brown, turning occasionally. Remove mushrooms from skillet. Increase temperature to moderately high (about 325° F.). Add beef slices a few at a time and cook until browned on both sides; remove beef as it browns. Reduce heat to moderately low (about 225° F.); place all the beef in the skillet and add mushrooms, soup, wine, water, dill, and pepper. Cover and cook until meat is fork-tender, about 40 to 45 minutes, stirring occasionally. Place buttermilk mixture and flour in a covered jar and shake until blended; stir into gravy in skillet and cook until heated, but do not boil. For diet serving allow 3 ounces of beef and ¼ of the sauce (about 10 tablespoons). About 285 calories. Serves 4.

Parsley Zucchini

4 small zucchini, sliced (about 1¼ pounds)	¾ teaspoon salt
1 tablespoon chopped parsley	¼ teaspoon dried tarragon leaves
1 tablespoon lemon juice	Pepper to taste
	½ cup water

Combine all ingredients in a saucepan and stir to mix well. Place over moderately high heat (about 275° F.) and bring to a quick boil. Reduce heat to low (about 200° F.); cover and simmer 15 to 20 minutes, or until crisp-tender. Drain. For diet serving allow ½ cup. About 10 calories. Serves 4.

Buttermilk-Herb Dressing

1 cup buttermilk	2 teaspoons finely chopped
1 tablespoon prepared mus-	parsley or 1 teaspoon
tard	dried parsley flakes
1 teaspoon instant minced	⅛ teaspoon dried dillweed
onion	⅛ to ¼ teaspoon salt
	Few grains pepper

Combine all ingredients in a jar with a tight-fitting cover. Shake to blend well. Chill several hours. Shake well before serving. Can be stored, tightly covered, in refrigerator about 1 week. About 7 calories per tablespoon. Makes 1 cup.

Friday / Menu 6

With Lunch at Home or to Carry / 1,189 Calories

BREAKFAST
1 cup fresh grapefruit sections
½ cup cooked cream of wheat
1 cup skim milk

LUNCH / AT HOME
Scrambled Eggs with Dried Beef
1 cup mixed green salad
1 tablespoon *Catsup Yoghurt
Dressing (see page 66)
1 slice whole wheat bread
1 unsweetened baked apple

LUNCH / TO CARRY
1 hard-cooked egg
1 slice pumpernickel spread with
1 tablespoon cream cheese
1 carrot, cut into sticks
½ stalk celery, cut into sticks
4 radishes
1 apple

DINNER
½ cup tomato juice
South American Lamb Stew
½ cup cooked noodles
15 inner chicory leaves
1 tablespoon *Catsup Yoghurt
Dressing (see page 66)
Orange Ambrosia

SUPPLEMENTS
1 cup skim milk
1 small banana
1 tangerine

* Recipe given

Scrambled Eggs with Dried Beef

1⅓ cups or 4 ounces dried beef

4 eggs

4 tablespoons milk

1 teaspoon butter or margarine

1 tablespoon chopped parsley

Paprika

Place dried beef in a strainer and rinse thoroughly under hot water. Dry well on paper towels. Beat eggs and milk with a fork until blended. Melt butter in a skillet over moderately low heat (about 225° F.). Add beef; cook and stir about 1 minute. Add eggs and parsley and cook, stirring frequently, until eggs are just set. Do not overcook. For diet serving allow ¼ of the scrambled eggs and beef mixture. Sprinkle with paprika. About 156 calories. Serves 4.

South American Lamb Stew

1 tablespoon vegetable oil

1¼ pounds cubed, boneless lean lamb

1 beef bouillon cube

¾ cup boiling water

⅛ teaspoon chili powder

¼ teaspoon ground ginger

½ cup chopped onion

1 clove garlic, finely minced

¾ teaspoon salt

1 16-ounce can tomatoes

1 tablespoon cornstarch

1 tablespoon water

Chopped parsley

Heat oil in a large skillet over moderately high heat (about 300° F.); brown meat on all sides. Drain off fat. Dissolve bouillon cube in the boiling water; add chili powder, ginger, onion, garlic, and salt. Pour marinade over meat and let stand 2 hours or longer to marinate, stirring occasionally. Put meat, marinade, and tomatoes in an oven-proof casserole. Place in oven preheated to 350° F. Bake 1½ to 2 hours, or until meat is fork-tender. Remove meat to serving dish. Blend the cornstarch and the 1 tablespoon water together. Gradually add to gravy, stirring vigorously. Place over moderately low heat (about 225° F.) and cook, stirring constantly, until thickened. Serve over meat. Sprinkle with chopped parsley, if desired. For diet serving allow 3 ounces of the meat and ¼ of the sauce. About 230 calories. Serves 4.

Orange Ambrosia

1 cup orange sections, about 3 medium-sized oranges

1 medium-sized banana, sliced

¼ cup flaked coconut

Combine all ingredients. Mix and chill until serving time. For diet serving allow ⅓ cup. About 66 calories. Serves 4.

Saturday / Menu 7
With Lunch at Home / 1,194 Calories

BREAKFAST
1 orange, sliced
½ cup cottage cheese
1 slice raisin bread

LUNCH
*Broccoli Custard
Relish plate: ½ carrot, cut into sticks, 1 stalk celery, and ¼ cucumber
1 slice water-packed pineapple

DINNER
*Quick Ham Divan
½ tomato, sliced
10 small inner chicory leaves
1 tablespoon *Buttermilk-Herb Dressing (see page 74)
½ grapefruit

SUPPLEMENTS
2 cups skim milk
1 apple

* Recipe given

Broccoli Custard

1 10-ounce package frozen chopped broccoli	Few grains pepper
1½ cups skim milk	4 eggs
2 tablespoons flour	¼ cup grated Parmesan cheese
1 teaspoon salt	

Cook broccoli according to package directions; drain and chop to cut up larger pieces of stalk. Drain very well between paper towels. Heat oven to 350° F. Place skim milk and flour in a covered jar and shake until blended. Pour milk mixture into a saucepan and cook over moderately low heat (about 225° F.) until thickened, stirring constantly. Remove from heat. Stir in salt and pepper. Beat eggs well and stir in Parmesan cheese. Add broccoli and milk sauce. Pour into a deep 1-quart casserole. Place casserole in a larger pan; add about 1 inch water to larger pan. Bake 65 to 70 minutes, or until a silver knife inserted in the center comes out clean. For diet serving allow ¼ of the casserole. About 163 calories. Serves 4.

Quick Ham Divan

1 9-ounce package frozen asparagus spears	1 tablespoon prepared mustard
11 slices cooked ham, about 1 pound, cut ⅛ inch thick	½ cup coarsely shredded mozzarella cheese

Heat oven to 325° F. Cook asparagus according to package directions; drain thoroughly. Spread ham slices with a thin layer of mustard. Place two asparagus spears at one of the narrow ends of the ham and roll up jelly-roll fashion. Arrange in a shallow, heat-proof serving dish. Bake ham rolls for 10 minutes; sprinkle with the cheese and continue baking 15 minutes. For diet serving allow 2 ham rolls and ¼ of the cheese topping. About 314 calories. Serves 4.

Sunday / Menu 8

With Lunch at Home / 1,195 Calories

BREAKFAST

½ cup orange juice
½ cup cooked farina
1 cup skim milk

LUNCH / AT HOME

*Skillet Frankfurters and
Sauerkraut
1 slice rye bread
1 pear

DINNER

½ cup tomato juice
*Veal Ragout
Relish plate: 2 radishes, 4 celery
sticks, and 5 carrot sticks
½ cup strawberry-flavored gelatin
with 1 slice water-packed
pineapple

SUPPLEMENTS

1 cup skim milk
1 apple

* *Recipe given*

Skillet Frankfurters and Sauerkraut

1 beef bouillon cube	1 1-pound can sauerkraut, drained
½ cup boiling water	1¼ cups boiling water
1 cup thinly sliced onion	2 cooking apples peeled, cored, and cut into wedges
½ teaspoon chili powder	
7 frankfurters	2 teaspoons sugar

Dissolve bouillon cube in the ½ cup boiling water. Add onion and cook over moderately low heat (about 225° F.) 5 minutes, until almost tender. Drain and stir in chili powder. Split frankfurters almost in half lengthwise and stuff with the onion mixture. Cover sauerkraut with the 1¼ cups boiling water and cook over moderately low heat (about 225° F.) 10 minutes. Add apple wedges and sugar; cook, covered, 10 minutes more. Drain and reserve liquid. Spoon sauerkraut mixture into skillet and add ¼ cup of the liquid. Arrange frankfurters over sauerkraut. Cover and cook over moderately low heat (about 225° F.) 10 minutes, until thoroughly heated. Add a little more of the reserved liquid if needed to keep sauerkraut moist. For diet serving allow 1 frankfurter and ¼ of the sauerkraut. About 248 calories. Serves 4.

Veal Ragout

1½ pounds boneless veal shoulder, cut into 1½-inch cubes	1¼ teaspoons salt
2 teaspoons vegetable oil	¼ teaspoon pepper
1½ cups boiling water	1½ cups sliced carrots
2 medium-sized tomatoes, coarsely chopped	1 cup sliced celery
½ cup chopped onion	2 medium-sized potatoes, peeled and diced
1 clove garlic, minced	1 9-ounce package frozen Italian green beans
½ teaspoon dried marjoram leaves	

Remove as much fat as possible from veal. Heat oil in a Dutch oven over moderately high heat (about 325° F.). Add meat a few pieces at a time and cook until all pieces are browned. Reduce heat to moderately low (about 225° F.); add boiling water, tomatoes, onion, garlic, marjoram, salt, and pepper. Cover and cook 1 hour. Add carrots, celery, and potatoes, and continue cooking 25 minutes longer, or until meat and vegetables are fork-tender. Add green beans and cook 10 minutes, stirring beans once so that they cook thoroughly. Skim off any fat. For diet serving allow 3 ounces of meat, ¼ of a potato, and ¼ of the vegetable-gravy mixture (a total of about ½ cup). About 277 calories. Serves 4.

Monday / Menu 9

With Lunch at Home or to Carry / 1,196 Calories

BREAKFAST

1 orange, sliced
1 ounce puffed wheat cereal
1 cup skim milk

LUNCH / AT HOME OR TO CARRY

*Scotch Broth
¼ cucumber
1 slice rye bread
1 tangerine

DINNER

*Chicken Marengo
½ cup cooked rice
*Brussels Sprouts with Basil
⅛ head lettuce
1 tablespoon *Buttermilk-Herb Dressing (see page 74)
½ cup water-packed dark sweet cherries

SUPPLEMENTS

1 cup skim milk
1 apple

* *Recipe given*

Scotch Broth

1 tablespoon vegetable oil	1 cup chopped celery
2 pounds lamb neck slices	stalks and leaves
6 cups boiling water	1 cup sliced carrots
1 bay leaf	1 cup sliced fresh green
2½ teaspoons salt	beans
⅛ teaspoon pepper	1 16-ounce can tomatoes
½ cup pearl barley	1 clove garlic, minced
½ cup sliced onion	¼ cup chopped parsley

Heat oil in a Dutch oven over moderately high heat (about 300° F.); brown lamb lightly. Drain off excess fat. Add water, bay leaf, salt, and pepper. Cover and simmer over low heat (about 200° F.) 1½ hours. Cool and chill several hours or overnight. Discard fat. Add barley. Cover; bring to a boil over moderately high heat (about 300° F.); reduce heat to moderately low (about 225° F.) and cook ½ hour. Add onion, celery, carrots, beans, tomatoes, and garlic; cook 45 minutes longer. Remove meat from bones, cut into large pieces, and place in soup. Stir in parsley just before serving. For diet

[79]

serving allow 1 cup of soup. About 206 calories. Makes about 2 quarts. Serves 4 to 5.

Chicken Marengo

1 2½-to-3-pound broiler-fryer chicken, cut into pieces
1 teaspoon salt
¼ teaspoon pepper
2 tablespoons flour
3 tablespoons butter or margarine
2 cloves garlic, chopped
½ cup water
1 8-ounce can tomato sauce
1 6-ounce can broiled mushroom crowns
1 tablespoon chopped parsley

Sprinkle chicken with salt and pepper, then with flour. Heat butter in a heavy skillet and brown chicken over moderately high heat (about 300° F.), turning frequently. Drain off fat from skillet. Add chopped garlic, water, tomato sauce, and juice drained from the mushrooms. Cook, covered, over moderately low heat (about 225° F.) 30 to 40 minutes, or until chicken is fork-tender. Add mushrooms and continue to heat until mushrooms are hot. Serve sprinkled with freshly chopped parsley. For diet serving allow 3 ounces of chicken and ¼ of the sauce. About 290 calories. Serves 4.

Brussels Sprouts with Basil

1 10-ounce package frozen Brussels sprouts
1 envelope instant chicken broth mix
¼ teaspoon salt
¼ teaspoon dried basil leaves
¾ cup water

Combine all ingredients in a small saucepan. Place over moderately high heat (about 275° F.) and bring to a quick boil. Reduce heat to low (about 200° F.). Cover and simmer 12 to 15 minutes, or until Brussels sprouts are crisp-tender, stirring occasionally. For diet serving allow ½ cup. About 25 calories. Serves 3 to 4.

Tuesday / Menu 10

With Lunch at Home / 1,192 Calories
With Lunch to Carry / 1,184 Calories

BREAKFAST

½ cup grapefruit juice
1 poached egg
1 slice raisin bread

LUNCH / AT HOME

*Celery soup
Bacon, lettuce, and tomato
sandwich (2 slices enriched white
bread, 2 strips cooked bacon,
½ sliced tomato, 1 lettuce leaf,
and 1 tablespoon *Catsup Yoghurt
Dressing (see page 66)
¾ cup water-packed fruits for salad

LUNCH / TO CARRY

*Celery Soup
Ham sandwich (2 slices whole
wheat bread, 2 ounces sliced
boiled ham, and 1 lettuce leaf)
½ cup grapes

DINNER

*Baked Stuffed Fish
½ cup cooked diced carrots
6 frozen asparagus spears, cooked
1 cup mixed green salad
1 tablespoon *Catsup Yoghurt
Dressing (see page 66)
1 apple

SUPPLEMENTS

2 cups skim milk
1 tangerine

*Recipe given

Celery Soup

1 cup water	¾ cup nonfat dry milk solids
1 teaspoon salt	2 tablespoons flour
Few grains pepper	1 teaspoon salt
2 cups diced celery	3 tablespoons grated onion
2 cups water	

Combine first 4 ingredients in a saucepan. Cook over moderate heat (about 250° F.) for about 10 minutes, until celery is just tender. Place the 2 cups water in the top of a double boiler; add dry milk, flour, and salt. Beat with a rotary beater until smooth. Add onion, celery, and the celery cooking water. Cook over moderately low heat (about 225° F.), stirring constantly, until mixture is smooth and thickened. For diet serving allow 1 cup soup. About 72 calories. Makes about 4 cups. Serves 4.

Baked Stuffed Fish

1 4-pound whole fish (red snapper, haddock, sole, or cod)	¼ cup chopped green pepper
4 tablespoons melted butter or margarine	¼ cup chopped celery
½ teaspoon salt	⅛ teaspoon garlic powder
⅛ teaspoon pepper	1 vegetable bouillon cube
¼ cup coarsely grated carrot	1 cup boiling water
	¼ cup chopped onion

Heat oven to 350° F. Brush fish inside and out with 2 tablespoons of the butter; sprinkle well with salt and pepper. Arrange in a large, flat baking dish. Cut deep crosswise gashes in the fish 1½ inches apart. Stir together the remaining 2 tablespoons butter, the carrot, green pepper, celery, and garlic powder. Spoon vegetable mixture into the gashes. Dissolve bouillon cube in the boiling water; add onion and cook over moderately low heat (about 225° F.) until onion is tender. Pour into bottom of baking dish around fish. Bake 55 to 60 minutes, or until fish is fork-tender. Serve pan juices over fish. For diet serving allow 3 ounces of the baked fish and ¼ of the vegetable mixture. About 281 calories. Serves 4.

Wednesday / Menu 11

With Lunch at Home / 1,188 Calories
With Lunch to Carry / 1,197 Calories

BREAKFAST
½ cup unsweetened pineapple juice
2 slices broiled Canadian bacon
1 slice whole wheat bread

LUNCH / AT HOME
*Garden Salad
½ cup cottage cheese
1 slice enriched white bread
1 apple

* Recipe given

[82]

LUNCH / TO CARRY

1 baked chicken breast
1 slice white bread
1 stalk celery
1 carrot
1 apple

DINNER

*Sherried Chicken Livers
½ cup cooked sliced carrots
*Italian Green Beans
Oregano
3 large romaine leaves
1 tablespoon *Buttermilk-Herb
Dressing (see page 74)
*Festive Broiled Grapefruit

SUPPLEMENTS

2 cups skim milk
1 orange

Garden Salad

1 quart crisp torn spinach leaves	2 tablespoons cider vinegar
1 cup sliced fresh mushrooms	2 tablespoons diced pimiento
½ teaspoon seasoned salt	

Toss all ingredients together in a salad bowl. Cover and chill about 1 hour before serving. For diet serving allow ¼ of the salad. About 51 calories. Serves 4.

Sherried Chicken Livers

1 pound chicken livers	1 4-ounce can mushroom stems and pieces, un-drained
2 tablespoons flour	
½ teaspoon salt	
⅛ teaspoon pepper	⅓ cup dry sherry
1 tablespoon butter or margarine	Pinch dried thyme leaves
¼ cup finely chopped onion	2 tablespoons chopped parsley

Wash and dry chicken livers well. Mix flour, salt, and pepper, and sprinkle over livers. Heat ½ the butter in a medium-sized skillet over moderately low heat (about 225° F.); add onion and cook until tender. Remove onion from skillet. Add chicken livers and the remaining butter and cook over moderately high heat (about 325° F.) for 5 to 8 minutes, or until livers are lightly browned. Reduce heat to moderately low (about 225° F.); add onion, mushrooms, sherry, and thyme. Cover and cook 10 to 12 minutes, or until

[83]

livers are cooked through. Serve garnished with chopped parsley. For diet serving allow 3 ounces chicken livers and ¼ of the vegetable-sherry sauce mixture. About 285 calories. Serves 4.

Italian Green Beans Oregano

1 9-ounce package frozen Italian green beans	2 tablespoons chopped onion
1 cup diced tomato (about 1 medium-sized tomato)	½ teaspoon salt
½ cup finely diced celery	¼ teaspoon dried oregano leaves
¼ cup finely diced green pepper	⅓ cup water

Combine all ingredients in a saucepan. Place over moderately high heat (about 275° F.) and bring to a quick boil. Reduce heat to low (about 200° F.). Cover and simmer 6 to 8 minutes, or until beans are crisp-tender, stirring and separating beans occasionally. For diet serving allow ½ cup. About 21 calories. Serves 4.

Festive Broiled Grapefruit

2 grapefruits	4 tablespoons flaked coconut

Cut grapefruits in half and remove cores. Cut around each section. Arrange halves in a shallow baking dish. Place under preheated broiler 3 to 4 inches from heat and broil about 4 minutes. Sprinkle with coconut and place under broiler for 2 minutes more, or until coconut is lightly browned. For diet serving allow ½ grapefruit. About 77 calories. Serves 4.

Thursday / Menu 12

With Lunch at Home or to Carry / 1,195 Calories

BREAKFAST	LUNCH / AT HOME
½ cup grapefruit juice	*Vegetable Salad Mold
1 cooked egg	½ cup cottage cheese
1 slice white bread	1 slice whole wheat bread
	1 small banana

* Recipe given

[84]

LUNCH / TO CARRY	DINNER

LUNCH / TO CARRY

*Chicken sandwich (2 slices whole
wheat bread, 3 ounces sliced
chicken, and 1 lettuce leaf)
1 stalk celery
½ carrot
1 tangerine*

DINNER

*¾ cup onion soup
*Chinese Beef
½ cup cooked rice
1 cup sliced Chinese cabbage
1 tablespoon *Buttermilk-Herb
Dressing (see page 74)
½ cup unsweetened applesauce*

SUPPLEMENTS

*2 cups skim milk
1 orange*

Vegetable Salad Mold

1 envelope unflavored gelatine	½ cup chopped fresh spinach
1¾ cups canned chicken broth	6 thin slices cucumber, halved
2 tablespoons lemon juice	½ cup sliced celery
¼ teaspoon salt	¼ cup thinly sliced radishes

Sprinkle gelatine over ¾ cup of the chicken broth in a small saucepan. Place over moderately low heat (about 225° F.) and heat until gelatine is dissolved, stirring constantly. Remove from heat and add the remaining 1 cup chicken broth, lemon juice, and salt. Chill until slightly thickened; stir in rest of ingredients. Pour into individual ½-cup gelatine molds and chill until set. For diet serving allow 1 mold. About 26 calories. Serves 4.

Chinese Beef

1½ to 2 pounds flank steak	½ cup thinly sliced celery
1 tablespoon vegetable oil	1 small green pepper, sliced
½ cup coarsely chopped onion	1 16-ounce can bean sprouts, drained
1½ cups canned beef broth	1 tablespoon cornstarch
2 tablespoons soy sauce	1 tablespoon water
½ teaspoon ground ginger	
1 cup thinly sliced carrots	
Few grains pepper	

[85]

Slice steak thin and remove as much fat as possible. Heat oil in a large skillet over moderately high heat (about 325° F.); add sliced steak a few pieces at a time and cook until slices are browned. Remove beef and reduce heat to moderately low (about 225° F.). Add onion and cook until tender, stirring occasionally. Return meat to skillet and add beef broth, soy sauce, ginger, carrots, and pepper; cover and cook 5 minutes. Uncover and add celery, green pepper, and bean sprouts; cover and cook 5 minutes. Mix cornstarch and water together. Stir into beef mixture and cook 4 to 5 minutes, until thickened. For diet serving allow 3 ounces of meat and ⅕ of the gravy mixture (about ½ cup). About 263 calories. Serves 5.

Friday / Menu 13

With Lunch at Home / 1,202 Calories

With Lunch to Carry / 1,189 Calories

BREAKFAST

½ cup orange juice
1 ounce corn flakes
1 cup skim milk

LUNCH / AT HOME

*Eggs à la Florentine
1 slice pumpernickel
1 stalk celery
1 small banana

LUNCH / TO CARRY

Tongue sandwich (2 slices
whole wheat bread and 3 ounces
sliced cooked tongue)
1 stalk celery
1 tangerine

DINNER

*Beef à la Mode
1 small boiled potato
*Green Beans and Celery
3 romaine leaves
1 tablespoon *Buttermilk-Herb
Dressing (see page 74)
Dried fruit compote: 2 cooked
unsweetened dried apricots and
2 cooked unsweetened dried prunes

SUPPLEMENTS

1 cup skim milk
½ grapefruit

* Recipe given

Eggs à la Florentine

⅔ cup skim milk

2 teaspoons flour

¼ cup coarsely shredded
Swiss cheese

¼ teaspoon salt

1 cup well-drained cooked
spinach

2 tablespoons shredded
Swiss cheese

2 eggs

Salt and pepper

Paprika

Heat oven to 375° F. Place skim milk and flour in a covered jar and shake until blended. Pour milk mixture into a small saucepan and cook over moderately low heat (about 225° F.) until thickened, stirring constantly. Add the ¼ cup Swiss cheese and salt, and heat until cheese is melted. Remove from heat. Spoon ½ cup spinach into each of 2 individual baking dishes. Make a hollow in center of spinach and sprinkle 1 tablespoon Swiss cheese over spinach in each dish. Drop an egg into each spinach hollow and sprinkle with salt and pepper. Pour half the sauce over the egg in each dish. Bake 15 minutes for a soft-cooked egg, about 5 minutes longer if a well-done egg is desired. Serve garnished with a sprinkling of paprika. For diet serving allow 1 dish. About 217 calories. Serves 2.

Beef à la Mode

1 3-pound lean beef bottom
round

1 cup canned beef broth

½ cup dry red wine

¼ cup wine vinegar

1 teaspoon salt

5 whole peppercorns

1 cup water

2 medium-sized onions, cut
into thin slices

1 clove garlic, minced

1 medium-sized carrot, sliced

1 bay leaf

¼ teaspoon dried thyme
leaves

8 medium-sized carrots,
scraped and left whole

2 16-ounce cans boiled
onions, drained

Place beef in a bowl. Mix together beef broth, wine, vinegar, salt, and peppercorns. Pour over meat; cover and refrigerate overnight. Remove meat from bowl and reserve marinade. Pat meat dry with paper towels. Heat oven to 350° F. Place Dutch oven over moderately high heat (about 325° F.); brown meat on all sides. Reduce heat to moderate (about 250° F.); add the water, marinade, onions, garlic, the sliced carrot, bay leaf, and thyme. Cover and bring to a boil. Place in oven and bake 2 hours. Drain meat juices from pan and discard bay leaf and peppercorns. Place meat juices and vegetables in an electric blender and blend at high speed. Pour back into Dutch oven and add the whole carrots. Bake 30 minutes more, or until meat and carrots are fork-tender; add onions and bake 15 minutes to heat. For diet serving allow 3 ounces of meat, ¼ cup gravy, 1 carrot, and ¼ cup onions. About 267 calories. Serves 4 to 6.

Green Beans and Celery

1 9-ounce package frozen French style green beans	⅛ teaspoon dried chervil leaves
1 cup diced celery	Pepper to taste
1 onion bouillon cube	¾ cup water
¼ teaspoon salt	

Combine all ingredients in a small saucepan. Place over moderately high heat (about 275° F.) and bring to a quick boil. Reduce heat to low (about 200° F.). Cover and simmer 8 to 10 minutes, or until beans are crisp-tender, stirring and separating beans occasionally. For diet serving allow ½ cup. About 16 calories. Serves 4.

Saturday / Menu 14
With Lunch at Home / 1,198 Calories

BREAKFAST

1 orange, sliced
1 poached egg
1 slice rye bread

LUNCH

3 ounces canned salmon
2 lettuce leaves
3 cucumber slices
4 radishes
½ carrot, cut into sticks
2 slices enriched white bread
½ cup unsweetened applesauce

DINNER

*Baked Lamb Chops
½ cup cooked yellow squash
½ cup cooked green beans
⅛ head lettuce
1 tablespoon *Catsup-Yoghurt Dressing (see page 66)
½ grapefruit

SUPPLEMENTS

2 cups skim milk
1 pear

* Recipe given

Baked Lamb Chops

4 shoulder lamb chops
(about 2¼ pounds)
Salt
½ cup coarsely chopped
onion
½ cup coarsely chopped
green pepper

1 16-ounce can stewed
tomatoes
½ teaspoon dried basil
leaves
1 teaspoon salt
⅛ teaspoon pepper

Remove as much fat as possible from chops. Heat oven to 350°F. Heat a medium-sized skillet over moderately high heat (about 300° F.) and sprinkle bottom with salt. Brown chops on both sides. Remove chops from skillet and arrange in a shallow 2-quart baking dish. Reduce heat to moderately low (about 225° F.). Add onion and green pepper to skillet and cook until tender, stirring occasionally. Add tomatoes, basil, the 1 teaspoon salt, and the pepper; heat until boiling. Remove from heat and pour over chops. Bake 1 hour, or until chops are tender. Skim off any fat from the tomato mixture. For diet serving allow 3 ounces lamb and ¼ of the sauce (about 6 tablespoons). About 248 calories. Serves 4.

Summer Slimming

THE summer version of the Wise Woman's Diet is also based on 1,200 calories a day and on the same principle of sound nutrition combined with enjoyable meals. These menus, however, have been planned especially for the summer and its many taste treats. You can lose pounds and still enjoy the season's bounty of fresh fruits and vegetables, as well as traditional picnic foods, including sandwiches. The Wise Woman's Diet can fit into almost any family's eating pattern and is a reducing plan you can follow all summer long.

Menu 1 / 1,210 Calories

BREAKFAST

½ small cantaloupe
1 poached egg
1 slice white bread

LUNCH

3 ounces tuna fish
2 leaves lettuce
2 slices whole wheat bread
1 peach

DINNER

½ cup tomato juice
1 lean lamb chop (2 x 1½ x ¾ inches)
½ cup cooked rice
½ cup cooked diced carrots
1 cup mixed green salad
1 tablespoon bottled low-calorie
French dressing
½ cup blueberries
¼ cup skim milk

SUPPLEMENTS

2 cups skim milk
3 fresh apricots
1 small banana

Menu 2 / 1,206 Calories

BREAKFAST

½ cup orange juice
1 ounce puffed wheat cereal
1 cup skim milk

LUNCH

1 frankfurter
¼ cup cottage cheese
½ tomato
1 cup mixed green salad
1 tablespoon bottled low-calorie
French dressing
1 nectarine

DINNER

½ grapefruit
3 ounces broiled bluefish
½ cup cooked sliced green beans
1 small baked potato
10 sprigs water cress
6 slices cucumber
1 tablespoon bottled low-calorie
French dressing
½ cup strawberries

SUPPLEMENTS

2 cups skim milk
3 fresh apricots
½ cup fresh cherries with stems

Menu 3 / 1,201 Calories

BREAKFAST
½ cup strawberries
1 ounce corn flakes
1 cup skim milk

LUNCH
Ham sandwich on whole wheat
bread with 3 ounces ham
1 cup mixed green salad
1 tablespoon bottled low-calorie
French dressing
3 fresh apricots

DINNER
3 ounces roast veal
½ cup cooked noodles
½ cup cooked diced carrots
1 cup sliced Chinese cabbage
1 tablespoon bottled low-calorie
French dressing
1 4-x-8-inch wedge watermelon

SUPPLEMENT
1 cup skim milk

Menu 4 / 1,200 Calories

BREAKFAST
½ cup orange juice
2 slices broiled Canadian bacon
1 slice whole wheat bread

LUNCH
½ cup cottage cheese
½ cup blueberries
½ peach
½ banana, sliced
Lettuce and water cress
1 tablespoon bottled low-calorie
French dressing
1 slice white bread
1 plum

DINNER
3 ounces steak OR roast beef
½ cup cooked peas
1 broiled tomato
3 large romaine lettuce leaves
1 tablespoon bottled low-calorie
French dressing
½ small cantaloupe

SUPPLEMENTS
1 cup skim milk
3 fresh apricots

Menu 5 / 1,186 Calories

BREAKFAST

½ grapefruit
⅔ cup cooked oatmeal
1 cup skim milk

LUNCH

½ cup cottage cheese
2-ounce slice boiled ham
Relish plate: 4 radishes, 5 carrot
sticks
2 slices whole-grain rye bread
1 plum

DINNER

1 cup jellied consommé
3 ounces broiled swordfish
½ cup cooked peas
½ broiled tomato
⅛ head of lettuce
1 tablespoon bottled low-calorie
French dressing
½ cup strawberries

SUPPLEMENTS

2 cups skim milk
½ cup fresh cherries with stems
1 peach

Menu 6 / 1,185 Calories

BREAKFAST

½ cup grapefruit
juice
½ cup cooked farina
1 cup skim milk

LUNCH

½ cup cottage cheese
6 cucumber slices
2 slices pumpernickel bread
1 cup strawberries

DINNER

1 cup consommé
1 lean lamb chop (2 x 1½ x ¾
inches)
1 small baked potato
½ cup cooked spinach
Relish plate: 2 radishes, 4 celery
sticks, 5 carrot sticks
1 cup fresh cherries with stems

SUPPLEMENTS

2 cups skim milk
1 apple
1 small banana

Menu 7 / 1,208 Calories

BREAKFAST

½ cup blueberries
1 ounce corn flakes
1 cup skim milk

LUNCH

3 ounces beef tongue
2 slices whole wheat bread
2 leaves lettuce
½ tomato
1 peach

DINNER

½ cup tomato juice
3 ounces broiled ham steak
1 small boiled potato
½ cup cooked spinach
Relish plate: 2 radishes, 4 celery
sticks, and 5 carrot sticks
½ small cantaloupe

SUPPLEMENTS

1 cup skim milk
1 plum
½ cup grapes

Menu 8 / 1,196 Calories

BREAKFAST

1 cup sliced peaches
⅔ cup cooked oatmeal
1 cup skim milk

LUNCH

3 ounces turkey OR chicken
2 slices white bread
2 leaves lettuce
½ tomato
1 tablespoon bottled low-calorie
French dressing
½ small cantaloupe

DINNER

1 cup consommé
3 ounces shrimp OR fish
½ cup cooked rice
½ cup cooked broccoli
1 cup mixed green salad
1 tablespoon bottled low-calorie
French dressing
½ cup blueberries

SUPPLEMENTS

2 cups skim milk
1 small banana
½ cup grapes

Menu 9 / 1,197 Calories

BREAKFAST

1 orange, sliced
½ cup cottage cheese
1 slice whole wheat bread

LUNCH

3 ounces chicken
2 slices white bread
2 lettuce leaves
½ tomato
1 tablespoon bottled low-calorie
French dressing

DINNER

½ cup tomato soup
3 ounces roast veal
½ cup cooked spinach
1 ounce French bread
Relish plate: 1 slice tomato,
3 slices cucumber, 1 stalk celery
1 cup fresh cherries with stems

SUPPLEMENTS

2 cups skim milk
1 nectarine

Menu 10 / 1,193 Calories

BREAKFAST

½ grapefruit
1 poached egg
1 slice white bread

LUNCH

3 ounces canned tuna
2 lettuce leaves
2 slices whole wheat bread
½ cup fresh fruit cup (pineapple,
banana, and orange)

DINNER

3 ounces broiled chicken
½ cup mashed cooked squash
½ cup cooked peas
⅛ head lettuce
1 tablespoon bottled low-calorie
French dressing
1 plum

SUPPLEMENTS

2 cups skim milk
1 small banana
1 pear

Menu 11 / 1,198 Calories

BREAKFAST

½ grapefruit
1 poached egg
1 slice white bread

LUNCH

3 ounces canned salmon
2 lettuce leaves
½ tomato
2 slices whole wheat bread
3 fresh apricots

DINNER

1 cup bouillon
3 ounces broiled chicken
1 small baked potato
½ cup cooked spinach
Relish plate: 2 radishes, 3 slices
cucumber, and 1 stalk celery
½ cup raspberry-flavored gelatin
1 peach, sliced

SUPPLEMENTS

2 cups skim milk
½ cup blueberries
1 4-x-8-inch wedge watermelon

Menu 12 / 1,201 Calories

BREAKFAST

½ cup grapefruit juice
1 poached egg
1 slice white bread

LUNCH

1 cup jellied consommé
½ cup canned lobster
5 carrot sticks
2 lettuce leaves
1 slice whole wheat bread
1 4-x-8-inch wedge watermelon

DINNER

3 ounces broiled beef liver
½ cup cooked Lima beans
1 5-inch ear corn, cooked
1 cup mixed green salad
1 tablespoon bottled low-calorie
French dressing
1 nectarine

SUPPLEMENTS

2 cups skim milk
2 plums
1 small banana

Menu 13 / 1,198 Calories

BREAKFAST
1 peach, sliced
1 ounce bran flakes
1 cup skim milk

LUNCH
1 slice bologna
1 slice liverwurst
2 tablespoons cottage cheese
2 romaine lettuce leaves
4 radishes
1 slice whole wheat bread
½ cup blueberries
¼ cup skim milk

DINNER
3 ounces lean roast loin of pork
½ cup cooked diced beets
½ cup cooked sliced green beans
Salad: ½ cup finely shredded
cabbage and ¼ green pepper, diced
2 tablespoons bottled low-calorie
French dressing
1 4-x-8-inch wedge watermelon

SUPPLEMENTS
1 cup skim milk
3 fresh apricots

Menu 14 / 1,157 Calories

BREAKFAST
½ grapefruit
⅔ cup cooked oatmeal
1 cup skim milk

LUNCH
3 ounces canned salmon
2 lettuce leaves
½ tomato
2 slices whole wheat bread
2 plums

DINNER
½ cup tomato juice
3 ounces boiled beef with horse-
radish
½ cup cooked cabbage
½ cup cooked diced carrots
1 pear

SUPPLEMENTS
1 cup skim milk
1 small banana
1 orange

THE
WISE WOMAN'S
EXERCISE PROGRAM

❀❀❀

Nine Body-Shaping Exercises

IF you are overweight and want a better figure, the combination of a sensible diet plan and exercise will provide long-term results. However, whether your figure is perfect, average, or poor, your body needs exercise to become —and stay—trim, lithe, supple, and shapely. The special shape-up program on the following pages will benefit your body in all those spots where pounds and inches pile up and settle through carelessness, sedentary living habits, and lack of exercise: hips, thighs, buttocks, waistline, and abdomen. Some of the nine body-shaping exercises are also beneficial as muscle toners for new mothers eager to regain their figures.

These nine exercises have been selected not only because they are pleasant and easy to do but also because they work. Success, though, comes only to the faithful. You need to spend at least ten minutes every day—the absolute minimum of time—on improving and keeping your figure. Whether those minutes are in the morning, afternoon, or evening, make them an established part of your routine—a daily exercise break. Performed regularly and conscientiously every day, these exercises will result in a definite figure improvement, and you should see pleasing contour changes after six weeks.

You'll probably take your exercises more seriously if you wear a leotard and tights, but any type of clothing that is comfortable and allows ease of movement can be worn. Begin your routine with two minutes of simple warm-up movements, such as stretching your arms up over your head, flopping the upper part of your body down from the waist in rag-doll fashion, doing half knee bends or arm swings. Not only will your muscles be more efficient if they are more limber, but also they will be much less liable to injury from sudden wrenches or strains.

Repeat each exercise sequence ten times; then select the one or two earmarked for your particular figure problems and give them special emphasis. Perform each movement with precision and concentration. Music is a pleasant accompaniment and can help you establish a more rhythmic precision. As you continue in the routine and your muscles strengthen, you may want to speed up your figure improvement by exercising longer.

This shape-up program will help correct body contours, but for all-around good health you also need some regular vigorous activity. Running, jogging, bicycling, riding, swimming, and tennis will help you to lose weight faster when combined with dieting and will increase your general physical fitness.

EXERCISES

THIGH TWIST

The *thigh twist* firms the muscles of your inner and outer thighs, trims buttocks, and discourages extra padding on your hips. It limbers up all the tight, inflexible muscles that are immobilized by sitting too much of the time. Stand with your feet about 12 inches apart, arms extended gracefully at the sides. Point your right toe, then twist the toe inward toward your other foot, the heel pointing outward. Twist your thigh until you can look down at the back of your right hip. Then turn the same toe outward, bending your knee and twisting your leg and hip in the opposite direction. Rest your heel flat on the floor so your feet are parallel, turned in opposite directions. Turn your head to look down your left arm. Do the same twist on the left side, and repeat the entire sequence ten times. Twist slowly, exerting pressure as you hold—briefly—the top of each inner and outer twisting motion.

WAIST TWIST

The *waist twist* can trim inches from your waistline—and help keep them off. Added benefits include making your neck more flexible and improving your chin-line. You can *feel* this exercise do its good work. Stand straight with your feet flat on the floor about 12 inches apart and your arms extended at your sides. Twist the upper part of your body as far to the left as you can, keeping your feet firmly planted on the floor and your hips in alignment straight across. Move only the upper part of your body as you twist. Turn your head in the direction of the twist and look down your left arm. Repeat the twist on the right side. Do ten twists on each side.

ROLL-DOWN

The *roll-down* (or roll-up) strengthens your abdominal muscles, allowing you to be fashionably firm and flat. It also is essential for building a strong back. One well-known exercise expert says that if she had to choose just one exercise to do every single day, this one would take top priority. Sit on the floor with your knees bent and your feet flat on the floor, held down under a low chest, chair, or footstool. Lock your hands behind your neck, press your elbows back, and roll slowly down to the floor. You should feel as if every vertebra is moving separately as you roll down. Then roll up very slowly just as you came down. Repeat ten roll-downs and roll-ups. If you find it too difficult to roll back up at first, start from scratch each time and do only the roll-downs until your muscles become stronger. As you grow more proficient at this exercise you will be able to keep your feet flat on the floor without the aid of a weight.

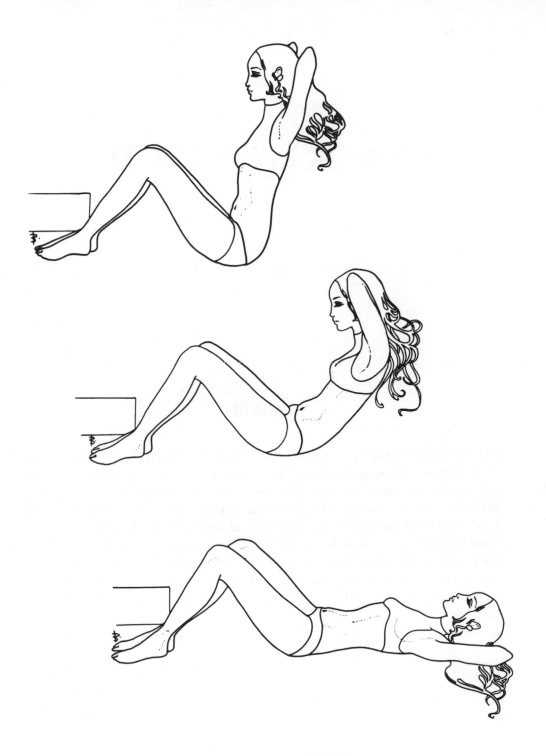

BACK STRETCH

The *back stretch* can do a lot toward trimming and reshaping the posterior. It also gives your legs, back, and abdomen a workout and makes your entire body more flexible. Another plus: It's an effective chin exercise. Grasping the back of a sturdy chair for support, stand about a foot away from it, round your back, bend your head downward and raise your right knee to meet your nose. Then swing your right leg back and up as high as you can as you straighten your knee, arch your back, and lift your head. Hold for a second, then return to the first position, and repeat the movement with your left leg. Don't swing your legs limply. Work to stretch them as far as possible each time. Repeat ten complete stretches with each leg.

[111]

THREAD THE NEEDLE

Thread the needle is an exercise designed to benefit your pectoral (chest) muscles, which in turn benefit the bosom. It also inhibits "spare tires" and fat upper backs and shoulders. Get down on all fours, knees apart, and rest your right shoulder and your head on the floor. Let your right arm lie along the floor toward the left. Support yourself with your left hand, with your left elbow bent. Draw your right arm back toward you and fling it outward and up as high as possible, following the movement with your head. "Thread the needle" with each arm ten times.

[113]

THE CAT

The *cat*, together with the next three exercises, has been recommended by doctors as part of a workout to help new mothers get back into shape. (You should always consult your own doctor before doing postpregnancy exercises.) And they are effective muscle toners and inch trimmers for every woman, whether she is a new mother or not. This exercise helps the pelvic area return to its normal state. Sit on your heels, then bend your body forward, and extend your arms in front, keeping your back flat. Push forward, to rest on hands and knees. Round your back like a cat and straighten your arms, tightening the abdominal muscles and pulling your back into an arc. Hold. Repeat the sequence ten times.

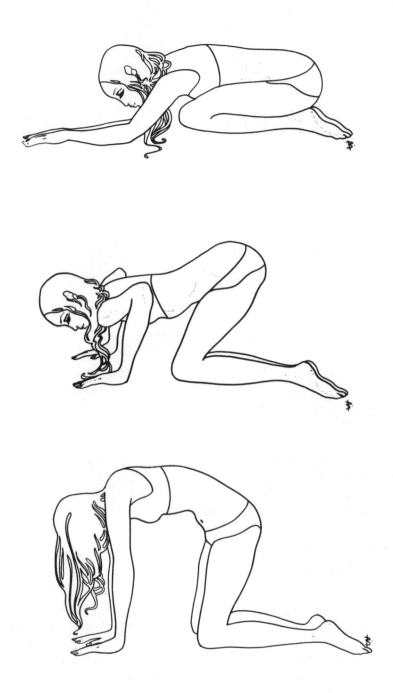

SIDE-TO-SIDE SHIFT

❀ ❀ ❀

The *side-to-side shift* is a gentle and restful exercise that helps coax a waistline back to its desired dimensions and also strengthens the lower back muscles. It is a favorite of new mothers in the process of regaining their prepregnancy figure and muscle tone. Lie flat on your back with both arms stretched out at your sides. With your legs together, bend your knees and raise them close to your chest, then drop them slowly to the left side and hold for a second. Bring them slowly back to your chest, then drop them slowly to the right side and hold. Be sure to press your lower back flat on the floor as you shift from side to side. Repeat ten times on each side.

[116]

KNEE-TO-NOSE STRETCH

The *knee-to-nose stretch* helps strengthen your abdominal muscles and back and streamlines your seat and the backs of your thighs. (This is essentially the same exercise as the back stretch, but the floor position emphasizes its benefits to both abdomen and back.) Get down on your hands and knees. Round your back, lower your head, and bring your left knee forward in an attempt to meet your nose. (It eventually will.) Stretch your leg slowly back and up as you lift your head. Repeat ten stretches with each leg.

LEG EXTENSIONS

Leg extensions produce strong, taut abdominal muscles and strengthen your back. This exercise is not as easy as it looks and must be accomplished in gradual stages. Do it at your own pace. Lie flat on the floor on your back, arms outstretched at your sides, your feet together. Bend your knees and bring them toward your chest in a relaxed position. Keeping your spine flat, straighten your knees, and stretch your legs straight up; hold briefly. Return to the bent-knee position and straighten your legs again, this time lowering them about six inches below the first position. Return to the relaxed bent-knee position and repeat the leg extensions, each time stretching them out a few inches lower than the previous time. Concentrate on your lower back. There must be no air space between you and the floor at this point. The lower the leg extension, the harder your abdominal muscles have to work. With your legs stretched out at the lowest position you can comfortably hold, bring your knees back toward your chest and repeat the extensions several times at that lowest level. As your muscles become stronger and more controlled, try for lower and lower levels. The goal is to be able to extend your legs just an inch or two above the floor and repeat the extensions ten times.

[119]